MW01428198

WISDOMS *and* AFFIRMATIONS

To Give You Wings To Soar

IRENE CABAY

BALBOA PRESS
A DIVISION OF HAY HOUSE

Copyright © 2016 Irene Cabay.

All rights reserved. No part of this book may be used or reproduced by any means, graphic, electronic, or mechanical, including photocopying, recording, taping or by any information storage retrieval system without the written permission of the author except in the case of brief quotations embodied in critical articles and reviews.

Balboa Press books may be ordered through booksellers or by contacting:

Balboa Press
A Division of Hay House
1663 Liberty Drive
Bloomington, IN 47403
www.balboapress.com
1 (877) 407-4847

Because of the dynamic nature of the Internet, any web addresses or links contained in this book may have changed since publication and may no longer be valid. The views expressed in this work are solely those of the author and do not necessarily reflect the views of the publisher, and the publisher hereby disclaims any responsibility for them.

The author of this book does not dispense medical advice or prescribe the use of any technique as a form of treatment for physical, emotional, or medical problems without the advice of a physician, either directly or indirectly. The intent of the author is only to offer information of a general nature to help you in your quest for emotional and spiritual well-being. In the event you use any of the information in this book for yourself, which is your constitutional right, the author and the publisher assume no responsibility for your actions.

Any people depicted in stock imagery provided by Thinkstock are models, and such images are being used for illustrative purposes only.
Certain stock imagery © Thinkstock.

Print information available on the last page.

ISBN: 978-1-5043-5237-6 (sc)
ISBN: 978-1-5043-5239-0 (hc)
ISBN: 978-1-5043-5238-3 (e)

Library of Congress Control Number: 2016905313

Balboa Press rev. date: 4/26/2016

Table of Contents

Introduction vii
Acknowledgments xi
The Courage to Change 1
Attitude 20
Calm Yourself 44
Gratefulness 55
Love 64
Ego 78
Infinite 83
Meditation 98
Points to Ponder 113
Lighten Up 120

Introduction

I was forty years old and going through one of the seemingly worst moments of my life. My husband of twenty-four years had just left me, and I felt as though my world had come crashing down. I had been a stay-at-home mom for most of those years and had only just begun to work part-time. I felt I had been tossed out of my cozy birdcage and left to free-fall into oblivion.

A few years later, my oldest son called on one of my particularly down days. After listening to me whine and cry over the phone, he said, "Mom, I'm going to send you a book and some cassettes. Maybe they will help." The book was by Dr. Wayne Dyer—"There Is a Spiritual Solution to Every Problem." The cassettes were by Jose Silva—*The Silva Mind Control*. I learned how to relax and meditate from a cassette series while learning to understand from a book that I *did* have control over my life. I then got Louise Hay's *I Can Do It* on CD and book. The book was my bathroom reader and the CD was my night-time lullaby. I fell asleep listening to her teaching me how I could change my life for the better through positive affirmations.

Within three months, people were commenting on how different I was. I was more cheerful. I looked younger. Unbeknownst to anyone else, even my business improved. My being tossed from the cage forced me to change my way of thinking and to realize that I had wings to soar to heights I had never imagined for myself. I thought that if this weird thinking—I call it *oobly boobly* stuff—worked so well and so fast, what would happen if I really applied myself?

I began to take notes of any inspirational sayings on bits of Post-it notes, napkins, and even corners of newspapers. I had scraps of paper all over the place. One day I realized that if all these notes had made a difference in my life at one time, they might be of value to me at a future time. I began to compile them into a notebook. The ideas and insights began to build on themselves. I tried to keep the words in the first person as much as possible, keeping it personal and not *out there* for someday or for someone else.

I believe all these wisdoms came to me at the perfect time in my life. Although some themes seem to be repeated throughout, I believe I did not get it the first time it was presented, hence the repetition. The universe is really good about letting me rewrite if I don't get it correct the first time.

Initially, I just wrote down things I heard or read with no regard for who said them or wrote them. Later I realized I have to give credit where credit is due if I want to receive the full benefit of the wisdom. So if this is something you may have said or written, I did not mean to steal it from you. I used it to help myself to become a better person. I thank you sincerely. I hope you understand my desire to share these wisdoms with others so that they can be transformed, as I was, into a better person, making for a better world.

Acknowledgments

Special thanks to my children, Len, Levi, and Sara, for helping me and inspiring me on my spiritual journey. Thank you to my husband, Ed, for supporting me in my decision to publish my notebook. Thank you to my parents, Walter and Joanna, who always told me I could be whatever I want to be. Thank you, Dr. Wayne Dyer. That one book changed my life. I went on to buy most of your books and was blessed to have seen you speak at a Hay House Conference in Denver, Colorado, just months before you passed to the other realm. You are missed. Thank you, Jose Silva, for guiding me through exercises to calm my drunken monkey brain. Thank you, Louise Hay. I continue to listen to *I Can Do It* in the car, at bedtime, and in waiting rooms. You continue to inspire me. And I thank my first husband for tossing me from the birdcage—to discover I have wings!

To my grandchildren, Chandler, Parker, Julian, Freya, Avery, Andi, and Shepard. May you learn these ideas and concepts early in life. You are more powerful than you realize.

The Courage to Change

The moment everything changed was when I realized I deserved so much better.

> *"It's impossible," says pride. "It's risky," says experience. "It's pointless," says reason. Give it a try," whispered the heart.*
> —Unknown

> *The first step toward getting somewhere is to decide that you are not going to stay where you are.*
> —Unknown

Do I really like the person I am becoming?

If no one told me who I was, who would I be?

> *Problems cannot be solved with the same level of thinking that created them.*
> —Albert Einstein

If I want things to change, I must think different thoughts, finding unfamiliar ways of approaching familiar subjects.

I cannot change a belief with less power than was used to create it.

Most people are more comfortable with old problems than new solutions.

When I live in despair, never taking responsibility for my gloom or changing lifelong patterns, it is a safe haven that allows me to suffer in comfort.

As I change, I often mourn the death of my old dysfunctional self because I was familiar with that unhealthy side of myself.

Once I know something, I cannot pretend I do not know again. I cannot go back to innocence, whether innocence is being naive or stupid.

Seeing differently is believing differently and leads to different ways of living.

Nothing happens until something moves.
—Albert Einstein

But where do I begin? Begin at the beginning. But where is the beginning? The beginning is now. I am here, and the time is now; therefore, I have begun.

There is no condition that cannot be reversed by choosing different thoughts. If I continue to focus as I have been, to think as I have been, and to believe as I have been, then nothing in my experience will change.

If what I am doing is not working, then I need to do something different.

To get something I never had, I have to do something I never did.

Think different, act different, live different.

What could I do? What should I do? What is the right thing to do? What am I willing to do? What does it boil down to?

Observe. Contemplate. Choose.

I want change but am frustrated and confused by new feelings. These feelings are really a result of my already having changed. It will take a while for others to accept the changes and mirror positive responses.

> *If you think you can or think you can't, either way you are correct. It's the thinking that makes it so.*
> —Henry Ford

Stop thinking about what I do not want, even if it is what is happening now. Ask myself what I want and change my thoughts to my intention (faster vibrations).

I cannot manifest health from "I abhor being sick," for I am ultimately thinking of sickness, and what I think about expands.

Some of the greatest accomplishments in the world were made by people who changed their minds.

Shift my energy from what is to the energy of what I want and what I intend to create, even if I do not have a clue how to do it.

Self-correction is like compound interest on a savings account; small changes add up to significant results. Failing to reflect is like interest on a credit card; small balances grow to a debt never to be repaid.

The universal power never judges or criticizes me. It only accepts me at my own value. Then it reflects my beliefs back to me.

> *What the mind can conceive and bring*
> *itself to believe, it can achieve.*
> —Napoleon Hill

If I am powerful enough to mess up everything I touch, everywhere I go, with amazing consistency, there must be a way to apply the same mental power in a more positive way.

Make my life the definition of what I believe about myself.

Act as though I am—and I will be.

When there is faith in the future, there is power in the present.

The future is not some place I am going to, but one I am creating. The paths are not to be found but made, and the activity of making changes both the maker and the destination.

My state of mind makes the difference. Today is a reflection either of the past or the beginning of my future. Which will it be? The choice is mine.

The mind sees pictures (not words); therefore, see it, crystallize it, and take the necessary steps to make it happen.

Five criteria of a well-formed intent: I really want it. I can imagine it. I deserve it. I take responsibility for it. Everyone benefits.

Know myself and what I want to create in my life; hold that in front of myself *always*.

> *The question is not what you look at, but what you see.*
> —Henry Thoreau

I feel_____, but I am willing not to be. Show me what I am not seeing.

See what I can see, not what I expect to see. Hear what I can hear, not what I expect to hear. Think what I can think, not what I expect to think.

Instead of being open to what I have and working to get what I want, do I use up all my power resisting what I have?

Eternity is not the hereafter … This is it. If I don't get it here, I won't get it anywhere.

> *Twenty years from now, you will be more disappointed by the things you didn't do than the ones you did do.*
> —Mark Twain

Only in this present moment can I create my future.

There is not enough time to do the things I want in life, so I should not waste any of that time on useless feelings of melancholy or self-pity.

When I am an old woman sitting in my rocking chair thinking about my life, what decision will I wish I had made?

Choose the path that makes for the best story.

> *The greatest force in the human body is the natural drive of the body to heal itself; but that force is not independent of the belief system. Everything begins with belief.*
> —Mother Theresa

Have more faith in the power to heal, not the disease.

My job is not to ask how but to say yes.

When I think something is impossible, I am giving more power to the (impossible) thought than I am to the solution, even if I do not know the solution at this point.

> *You are full of heavenly stuff and bear the inventory of your best graces in your mind.*
> —Shakespeare

My mind is the substance of all matter.

Law of energy—like attracts like. What am I attracting? Maybe I need to change.

The Courage to Change

> *Sell your cleverness and purchase bewilderment.*
> —Rumi

Refuse to *pursue* happiness; instead, *bring* happiness to all I undertake. Joy is found realizing it is within me.

> *There is only one reason why you are not experiencing bliss at this present moment, and it is because you are thinking or focusing on what you do not have.*
> —Anthony DeMello

By focusing on what is wrong or missing, I miss experiencing bliss.

What does this closed door mean? Do I simply need to persevere, try a new approach, or look for something new?

Every miracle begins with a problem.

All of my errors, mistakes, and flaws occurred because they had to—so that I could transcend them.

If I could know in the midst of suffering that the experience was a necessary prelude to a spiritual advance, then I could rejoice in the suffering.

> *Even as a tortoise draws in its limbs, the wise can draw in the senses at will.*
> —Sri Krishna

Treat negative thoughts as if an external person, whose mission is to make my life miserable, uttered them.

A simple yes or no—nothing else satisfies the mind. It has to know what is real or it lives its life trying to prove what it thinks, never being able to rest.

Every thought pretends that it matters so much and wants to draw my complete attention. Do not take my thoughts too seriously.

Will it matter in ten minutes, ten years? The more I practice perspective, the less I will be knocked over by every bump in the road.

Thoughts mistake opinions and viewpoints for truth.

My beliefs are actually addictions.

Excuses are lies that I tell myself—and believe.

It takes practice to create a new pathway.

> *What if I woke up and every single day I did everything within my ability during that day to change my life? What could happen in just a month, a year? What would be different about my life?*
> —Liz Murray

True nobility is not about being better than anyone else; it is about being better than I used to be.

I do not claim perfection; I claim progress.

It is better to do the best I can, rather than the most I can.

My mental attitude determines my experience.

I work and sacrifice for the cause of fulfillment.

In order to find a more purposeful life, I must let go of what society and people think of me and look inside myself through some discipline—prayer and meditation—to find out what matters most to me and pursue it.

It takes courage to endure the sharp pains of self-discovery rather than choose to take the dull pain of unconsciousness that could last the rest of my life.

I would rather suffer the pain of discipline than the pain of consequences.

Sometimes the pain of letting go is less than the pain of hanging on.

> *Everything can be taken from a man but one thing: the last of human freedoms—to choose one's own way.*
> —Viktor Frankl

Chained by my certainties, I become a slave; I lose my freedom.

One must be cautious not to have spent one's life doing neither what one ought or what one likes; doing *nothing*. *Nothing* is strong enough to steal one's best years, not in sin but in a dreary flickering of the mind over it knows not what and knows not why—in gratification of curiosities so feeble that one is only half aware of them—with no lust or ambition to give one relish and too weak and fuddled to shake it off.

Distractions lead to doubt and lack of faith, and they stop the flow of blessings.

Fear of discovery pushes me into blind acts of busywork. It is quite a chore to keep my mind busy enough in labor and fantasy to avoid knowing consciously what I know inside.

Everything I do is based on the choices I make. It is not my parents, my past relationships, my job, the economy, the weather, an argument, or my age that is to blame. I, and only I, am responsible for every decision and choice I make. Period.

This is the only moment I have.

> *Man is not fully conditioned and determined but rather determines himself whether he gives in to conditions or stands up to them. In other words, man is ultimately self-determining. Man does not simply exist but always decides what his existence will be, what he will become in the next moment.*
> —Viktor Frankl

Only humans have the ability to create/change external events and circumstances. My thoughts and emotions (uniquely human traits) determine if it will be better or worse.

How do I want to be perceived? I want to be seen as a _____ person.

No one takes anything away from me unless I give it up first.

If I do not follow my own thoughts, then I will follow the thoughts of the fellow who followed his.

I will not get anywhere if I do not know where I am going.

I can make a living or design a life.

I do not have to survive. When merely concerned with survival, maintaining status quo, I strive for a reputation that stifles progress and becomes self-limiting.

> *What the caterpillar thinks is the end of the world,*
> *the butterfly knows is only the beginning.*
> —Unknown

Sometimes the strings of my past are burned because I need a new beginning.

The expert in anything was once a beginner.

> *The heart runs on inspiration, the mind functions on*
> *words alone. Passion defies gravity and gives wings to*
> *the heart. How high are you willing to climb?*
> —Peter Ragnar

The joy is having something to aim for.

If I believe in what I am doing and if I am not hurting other people, then I can be fearless.

Have the disciple to listen to my heart—and then have the courage to follow.

Action without vision is simply using up my time, but vision without action is only a daydream.

If we listened to our intelligence, we'd never have a love affair. We'd never have a friendship. We'd never go into business because we'd be cynical. That's nonsense. You've got to jump off cliffs all the time and build your wings on the way down.
—Ray Bradbury

It's better to look back on life and say, "I can't believe I did that," than to look back and say, "I wish I did that."

I am no longer accepting the things I cannot change. I am changing the things I cannot accept.
—Angela Davis

Do not fight the world that is; create the world that could be.

Focus! Focus! Focus! Where am I in my life? What am I doing to make things better? Where am I going?

If I get lost, it does me no good to think about where I started from. I must focus on how to arrive at my destination from where I am now. Likewise, with goals in life, determine the best way to get them from where I am now. Fretting about my past will not move me forward; it will only keep me fixed in the past.

Let go of a past I cannot change.

Guilt immobilizes. Focus on the idea of a solution to access a spiritual solution.

It is never too late or too early to be whoever I want to be.

Unless I first understand what I need, I cannot know what I need.

Identify my true needs and then make it a priority to pursue them.

> *You can have anything you want if you want it desperately enough. You must want it with an inner exuberance that erupts through the skin and joins the energy that created the world.*
> —Sheila Graham

What my mind naturally gravitates toward is what I worship.

I project outward what I feel inward. I resent when I feel resented. I judge when I feel judged.

Live a life that expresses my values.

I do not go around feeling moral or honest—I just am.

> *Continuous effort—not strength or intelligence— is the key to unlocking our potential.*
> —Sir Winston Churchill

The road to success is uphill all the way.

If it is not exceptional, it is not acceptable (work ethic).

Is the activity I am involved in going to give me a return on my time, equal to or greater than my hourly worth?

Make the plan; go until it is done.

> *You have to bite it in order to taste it.*
> —Pierre Dion *(regarding life)*

To leave no regrets at the end of my life, I must live with courage, moving toward what I want rather than away from what I fear.

Give me the courage to fail, for if I have failed, at least I have tried.

Change is the price I pay for progress.

> *There is no problem in any situation that faith will not solve.*
> —A Course in Miracles

The future can be reprogrammed in this moment. I do not need anyone's approval. Simply ask for a miracle and allow it to happen. Do not resist it.

I will always receive help within a second of a prayer. To recognize the help, I must see everything in my life from that second on as part of the answer to my prayer.

If I find out that what I fear is, at most, illusions of my mind only, then I have identified where I will develop next. Eradication of the fear, with the introduction of spirit, cannot live in the same space. Recognizing the nothingness, appearing as a problem, is what frightens me.

Instead of fighting darkness, bring in light.

When I turn and look directly at my fears, what I face dissolves in the light of consciousness.

> *When the winds of change blow, some build walls and others build windmills.*
> —Chinese Proverb

Sin (meaning *off the mark*) can lead to misguided energy (guilt, shame, and anxiety over whether God will forgive me). It is only a behavior that is an obstacle to finding my spiritual solution.

Sin should be viewed in the context of an obstacle that I have yet to overcome; it can be empowering.

Settle my problems as promptly and as thoroughly as I am able.

If I do not deal with the problem, I will become what I detest.

Once I bring correction to the problem, the problem loses validity and therefore disappears.

Correct the error in my thinking that produces the problem in the first place.

Thinking is the source of my problems.

I can only experience problems in my mind.

> *Change is hard at first, messy in the middle, and gorgeous at the end.*
> —Robin Sharma

In the same way I have learned to work with the nature of fire, I can learn how to work with suffering in my life.

What can determine my happiness in life is the step I take after a setback.

Do not use circumstances as a crutch; this will only hold me back.

I am a product of my environment. I need to find a way out or adjust as best I can.

I can't cure a chipped plate. All I can do is live with it or throw it out.

All pain simply comes from a futile search for what I want, insisting where it must be found.

Let go and let God. Let go of my sense of taking responsibility for everything and everyone around me.

Let go or be dragged.

> *We begin to prepare for the work that we have to do and customarily we have no idea what we are preparing for.*
> *—Peace Pilgrim*

> *Yet, it is only when the work is done that the meaning of the creative effort can appear and that the development of the artist brought about by it is attained.*
> *—The Creative Process: A Symposium* (Brewster Ghiselin)

Sometimes it is not enough to do my best; I must do what is required.

What can I do today? Can I go to bed knowing more than I did when I woke up? Did I leave more than I took?

What is my intention behind the action/words?

Forget myself in the consumption of the moment; do something challenging that requires competency and has a clear goal. What matters is the process of doing rather than the reward.

The legacy I leave is the life I lead. Live my life daily and leave my legacy daily—not some grand plan but little decisions daily—because I never know what impact things will have or when I may have an impact.

Be impeccable with my word. Speak with integrity. Say only what I mean. Avoid using words to speak against myself or gossip about others. Use the power of my word in the direction of truth and love.

Do not take anything personally. Nothing others do is because of me. What others say and do is a projection of their own reality, their own dream. When I am immune to the opinions and actions of others, I will not be the victim of needless suffering.

Do not make assumptions. Find the courage to ask questions and to express what I really want. Communicate with others as clearly as I can to avoid misunderstandings, sadness[,] and drama. With this one agreement, I completely transform my life.

Always do my best. My best is going to change from moment to moment; it will be different when I am healthy as opposed to sick. Under any circumstance, simply do my best and I will avoid self-judgment, self-abuse[,] and regret.
—The Four Agreements (Don Miguel Ruiz)

If that child ... could endure, alter, and survive that situation without any help, professional training, coaching,

> *or college degree, let alone a great deal of practical experience, what is stopping you from achieving your desires?*
> —*A Child Called "It"* (Dave Pelzer)

Do not be ruled by fear.

Rehashing negative events tarnishes the present moment by proxy.

True change is within; leave the outside as it is.

Only I can control my thoughts.

> *The best time to plant a tree was twenty years ago.*
> *The second best time is today.*
> —Chinese proverb

What do I wish I had learned sooner?

If I could go back in time, what advice would I give to my younger self?

What is the best advice I ever got? Did I take the advice? How have I used it?

What was a major crossroads in my life? Times that I went this way or that? What difference did that decision make in terms of how my life turned out?

What does not matter? Want do I wish I had paid less attention to?

What am I most certain matters a great deal if a person wants to find happiness and live a fulfilling life?

What role has spirituality played in my life?

How do I feel about my mortality? Am I afraid of dying?

What is the greatest fear at the end of my life?

Finish the sentence: I wish I had _____.

> *I want to create a life I do not need a vacation from.*
> —Sara Bellemore

Attitude

All the good things that God has conspired to make me deliriously happy are coming to me now, in the perfect way and through grace, and I receive them for my good and the good of others. Everything that is contrary to my highest good is leaving me now, and I happily let it go.

I attract only those who are in alignment with the highest ideals for myself.

Day by day, in every way, I am becoming more successful.

> *Stop wearing your wishbone where your backbone ought to be.*
> —Elizabeth Gilbert

Motivate myself by asking, "What would really bring me happiness now?"

Attitude

If I think toward worry, think the worst first and then plan to create the best outcome.

We must not, in trying to think about how we can make a big difference, ignore the small daily differences we can make which, over time, add up to big differences that we often cannot foresee.
—Marian Wright Edelman

Am I better than I was yesterday?

If I learn from everything I see, I will gain power from it.

Knowledge has to be improved, challenged, and increased constantly or it vanishes.

If the means do not contribute to the human happiness, neither will the end.

Limit my exposure to negative circumstances and, if possible, make the best of them.

Money does not measure my success. The people I meet and the influence in my life will be my success.

The little things in life determine the big things.
To have an excellent life, strive for an excellent year.
Within that year, strive for an excellent month.
Within that month, strive for an excellent day.
Within that day, strive for an excellent hour.
An excellent life is the sum of many excellent moments.
—MaryAnne John

What brought/brings me the most happiness in life—the greatest joy moment to moment?

What has brought me the greatest sense of meaning and purpose in life?

Why does it matter that I am alive?

Be brutally honest. Practice conscientious self-inquiry to deepen my understanding of who I am, what I am doing, and why. Be in touch with both my stated intentions and my less obvious intentionality, my hidden and often subconscious motivations.

Now that I know better, I can do better.

Apply myself with enthusiasm for what I will accomplish.

Attempt the impossible until it becomes an everyday part of my life.

Practice and take time to cultivate a positive attitude.

Excellence does not require perfection.

> *Letting things go is an act of far greater power*
> *than defending or hanging on.*
> —*A New Earth* (Eckhart Tolle)

What stands in my way? Am I ready to release it?

Would I rather hold the grudge or be happy?

I must want something more than my grudge in order to be willing to let it go.

Whether I blame or complain or not, things stay the same. Spend that energy on something useful, positive, uplifting.

Peace is the result of retraining my mind to process life as it is, rather than what I think it should be.

I can only lose something that I have; I cannot lose something that I am.

Arguing for my limitations is just resistance. In addition, resistance is just a delay tactic. It is another way of saying that I'm not good enough to have what I am asking for.

If I feel guilty about something, make amends as best I can. Turn it around and use it as a stepping stone to make things better.

Do I spend more time and energy complaining about something than it took for the situation to happen?

Doers have no time to criticize.

It's not worth it to spend one hundred dollars on a five-cent irritation.

Throw out the garbage in my life like the trash, then wash my hands and forget it.

If I can obtain it overnight, I can lose it just as quickly.

We don't see things as they are; we see them as we are.
—Anais Nin

I stopped checking for monsters under my bed when I realized they were inside me.

Everything vibrates; everything moves. The vibrations contain no evil, no problems. Only when my ears hear it or eyes see it do I perceive the *problem.*

It is how I choose to process the events, not the events themselves, which determines my level of peace.

Listen not only to what is said but also to the message behind the words.

Anger is just an energy, a reaction; it is workable. It has something to tell me, if I listen.

External events always reflect back to me my inner state.

I am never upset for the reason I think.

My mind forms my inner landscape and outer circumstances.

What is the myth that is holding me back from feeling the maximum happiness right in this moment?

Problems only reveal where my faith is.

Only what I am not giving is lacking. (For example, the world isn't boring; I am boring.)

Attitude

I do not attract what I want; I attract what I am.

I attract what I am feeling!

> Reputation is made in a moment;
> character is built in a lifetime.
> Building character takes focus and patience,
> with attention to detail and an ability to be consistent over time.
> While God is our potter,
> I also play the role of potter in forming my own character.
> The more stressed I am,
> the less likely I am to create a character of beauty.
> —MaryAnne John

Be more concerned with my character than my reputation, for my character is what I really am; while my reputation is merely what others think I am.

Be careful of my thoughts because my thoughts become my words; my words become my actions; my actions become my habits; my habits become my character; and my character becomes my destiny.

My job is to tend to my growth as a person—my grace, integrity, and humility. I need no other goal. The core of my being then grows into a substantial power, externally as well as internally.

Making my goal anything other than peace is emotionally self-destructive. If I make peace my goal, then if I get the job, raise, or boyfriend, that is great; but if I do not, I am still peaceful.

Change it with grace. Leave it with grace. Accept it with grace.

The more gracefully I behave, the less havoc I leave in my wake.

When I have the urge to give unrequested advice (aloud or in my mind), ask myself, "Whose business am I in? Did anyone ask for my opinion? Can I know what is right for someone else?" Then listen to my own advice and know that I am the one for whom it is meant.

When I *do* or *think* onto others, I really *do* and *think* it into my character (unto myself) via the sub-conscious. I auto-suggest it to myself.

I become what I judge.

The world is a mirror that reflects my character back to me.

> *Ability will enable a man to go to the top,*
> *but it takes character to keep him there.*
> —MaryAnne John

Being honest is very easy when I am not afraid of losing something.

I cannot make the same mistake twice. The second time it is a choice.

> *Experience is not what happens to a man; it is what*
> *a man does with what happens to him.*
> —Aldous Huxley

Experience is a teacher that knows no favorites.

Attitude

To dare is to lose my footing temporarily. To not dare is to lose my life.

The seed of success is dormant in every defeat.

I can either work through anxiety or become a slave to it.

The past has no power to stop me from being present now; only my grievance about my past can do that.

Flap my wings and let it go. Release the emotion, the story, and the hurt.

A little bit of adversity can help me realign myself, make me humble, and make me strive harder.

If I always won at everything, life would become boring. The test of my ability is what makes it all worthwhile.

Attitude is the determining factor of whether my failures make me or break me.

I cannot cause the wind to blow the way I want, but I can adjust my sails so that the wind will take me to where I want to go.

Do not pray for no rivers in life; pray for bridges.

Hopelessness is a real cause of failure.

A man is half-whipped the minute he begins to feel sorry for himself or to spin an alibi with which he would explain away his defeats.

The only way to fail is to give up.

To accept failure as final is to be finally a failure.

Do not draw a curtain too soon. There is always an encore or a fourth act.

Poverty is the richest experience that can come to a man; however, get away from it as quickly as possible.

> *The world has a habit of making room for the man whose words and actions show that he knows where he is going.*
> —Napoleon Hill

There is nothing more attractive than someone with passion for something, who looks at things positively and is always seeking to better himself or herself.

Focus. Where am I? What am I doing? Where am I going?

What would happen if I saw life as something to be savored rather than as a series of problems to be solved?

Throw my heart over the bar and my body will follow.

If I am not willing to learn, no one can help me. If I am determined to learn, no one can stop me.

> *Whatever you can do, or dream you can, begin it.*
> *Boldness has genius, power[,] and magic in it.*
> —William Hutchison Murray

Attitude

State the problem. Ask for a specific answer. Believe that I am getting that answer. It will rush in like a tide.

Before I quit on myself when life is not fair, exhaust all my options for making things happen.

Do *something* to manage my destiny.

Acquire a quiet sense of inner determination.

I am going to get out what I stand for.

It is my life and my choice.

> *Don't make me walk when I want to fly.*
> —Galina Doyla

Expressing my full potential is more than my right—it is my responsibility.

> *Do just once what others say you can't do and you will never pay attention to their limitations again.*
> —James R. Cook

Rather than trying to talk people into believing, it's better to reveal the radiance of my own discovery.

> *If I don't think highly of myself, why should anyone else think highly of me?*
> —Loretta Skarsen

My opinion is of value. I deserve to be heard.

Take pride in how far I've come. Have faith in how far I can go.

I have people's approval of me when I need it. In either case, it has nothing to do with me. It is only their story of me that they are approving of.

Do not look at myself through a fun-house mirror, distorted by others' programming since birth. That is not who I am.

There are only two keys that determine who I am: who I conceive myself to be and who I associate with.

Do not give myself away in the vain hope of appeasing others.

I can please others without giving away myself in the process. When I please others in the hope of being accepted, I lose my sense of self-worth.

> *I will not let anyone walk through my mind with their dirty feet.*
> —Gandhi

Shoulds only get in my way. Just notice and choose the other option.

Do not allow crap under my skin and into my head.

Disinfect myself, scrape it off, and move on. I have no control over it anyway.

> *It is better to walk alone, than with a crowd going in the wrong direction.*
> —David Avocado Wolfe

Attitude

Rather than expect things from others, aspire to my own goals and dreams.

Make and maintain the commitment of being my own person.

When I shrug off my duty to myself, I am still living in the shadow of my controller.

The pain I might experience by others' reaction to my spreading my wings is nothing compared to the pain of my clipping them.

I must control my environment, thereby insuring myself against the influence of a negative environment.

A pessimist is the same as a burglar. He will rob me of joy.

> *Attitude defies limitation and exceeds expectation.*
> —Unknown

Instead of expanding my ability to go out and get anything, expand my ability to receive what is already here for me.

Too many people put their faith in others rather than in themselves or what is in front of them and readily available.

By accepting myself exactly as I am and where I am, I have more energy to give to life; I am not wasting my time trying to make things different.

Why travel across the desert if the well is right in from of me?

If I am doing all that I can without a sense of joy or even satisfaction, there is a strong chance I may not get to where I want to go.

Be content in material areas, as they are limited by boundaries. The spiritual realm, however, is unlimited.

Power produces imitation.

> *Excellence is not a skill. It is an attitude.*
> —Ralph Marston

Attitudes are more important than facts.

A promotion will not give me an outstanding attitude, but an outstanding attitude will give me a promotion.

Heroes are just as afraid as the rest of us, but they have learned to confront and walk through their terrors.

To refuse to think of myself as limited in any way is to see my spirit as perfect and always connected to God, regardless of any bodily impairment (for instance, consider Stephen Hawking).

Magellan may have rounded Cape Horn, but I can be as brave just sitting in my living room.

Do not leave my happiness to fate.

When I hit the bump in the road, it is only the bump in the road.

Lift myself out of the rough by keeping my eyes fixed firmly on the source of my power.

Your only limitation is the one that you set up in your own mind.
—Napoleon Hill

Changing how I think can change my outcome.

I move through life creating experiences to match my beliefs.

Look around less and imagine more.

There is never enough of *more* (as long as it is based on positive).

It is mind over matter—do not mind all the crap out there because none of it matters.

Imagination is more important than knowledge. Knowledge is limited. Imagination encircles the world.
—Albert Einstein

Contemplation is the highest form of activity.

Children think with their feelings. When our minds mature, we learn to cover our feelings with sophisticated thoughts, which is only a form of denial.

Forced idleness is far worse than forced labor. Being forced to work, and forced to do your best, will breed in you temperance and self-control and strength of will and content and a hundred other virtues which the idle will never know.
—Napoleon Hill

Idleness will cause atrophy of willpower.

The more often I feel without acting, the less I will ever be able to act and ultimately the less I will be able to feel.

If I want it, I have to be willing to pay the price.

> *Hard work and determination will always surpass skill and laziness.*
> —Levi Bellemore

The wrong attitude will hinder my progress, regardless of how hard I work.

Work hard and intelligently.

Constructive criticism equals knowing mine as well as others' capabilities and expecting nothing less.

> *Pain is just weakness leaving the body.*
> —Levi Bellemore

When in pain, remember there is light beyond this darkness. What goes on externally is only the tip of the iceberg. The lessons, the real changes, are things my eyes cannot see. They lie beneath the spiritual waterline of my soul's journey.

Sometimes it takes the knife that emotionally pierces my heart (painful lessons and experiences) to break through the walls that lie in front of it.

In times of trauma, loss, or fear, look to a world not defined by pain in order to heal; try to find a context of still existing goodness.

Remember what really matters to me; put aside the hurt and move on.

> *Life is suffering. Attachment is the source of suffering.*
> *The end of attachment will bring the end of suffering.*
> —Buddha

Expectations kill happiness, whether I get what I want or not.

When I expect or demand that life be fair, I impede the process toward resolution and/or healing and therefore get stuck.

Refuse to wait for a pay-off that may never materialize.

Reducing expectation promotes contentment. The extra energy can be used to devote to meditation and to achieve cessation of problems.

I can't reach for anything new if my hands are filled with yesterday's junk (regret, guilt, hurt, anger, fear).

When I choose not to see what is in front of me, I have seen anyway. I saw, I denied, and I slipped deeper into my hidden world, feeling lonely and full of fear, yearning to be happy, joyous, and free.

All negative desires are nothing but frustrations of positive desires inspired by defeat, failure, or neglect by me to adapt to nature's laws in a positive way.

Beautiful things happen in my life when I distance myself from the negative.

Outside influence can only help me so far.

Some become slaves to the outlets and are controlled all over again (addiction). It is not my external but internal environment that counts.

Problems are illusions of the material world.

I do not have to take finite (worldly) games seriously.

> *It is not what you say out of your mouth that determines your life. It is what you whisper to yourself that has the most power.*
> —Robert Kiyosaki

Let the doctors handle my body. Let God handle my life. But be in charge of my own moods.

Be aware of *normal* suffering—irritation, impatience, anger, complaining.

If I create suffering for myself, I am probably creating suffering for others too.

I cannot be aware *and* create suffering at the same time.

Attitude

Accept what is. If I am angry, then accept that I am angry. Accept my non-acceptance.

> *You become what you think about most of the time.*
> —Earl Nightingale

What I think about I bring about.

See myself surrounded by the conditions I wish to create.

Consistently keep myself in check with the environment that I create.

I will turn into the thing I pretend to be, whether optimist or cynical, patriot or pacifist.

In my world, nothing ever goes wrong.

> *If you have good thoughts[,] they will shine out of your face like sunbeams and you will always look lovely.*
> —Roald Dahl

Happiness is as contagious as gloom.

Put my energy and attention on what I am *for*.

Would I rather be right or would I rather be happy?

When I shift my thoughts, my emotions follow suit—then my behavior, positively and negatively.

Always dress and look like the kind of person I want to be.

WISDOMS and AFFIRMATIONS

One's destination is never a place but a new way of seeing things.
—Henry Miller

Karma is like the wind of outer and inner, material and mental conditioning. I cannot control the wind, but I can choose to sail and navigate skillfully.

Denial is an admission that something is wrong with me.

What is one positive thing I can do now that will improve this situation?

My acts are always in harmony with the dominating thought of my mind.

Reprogram my negative thoughts into positive ones.

Positive thought habits, controlled by myself, serve my aims and purpose, in addition to the privilege of self-determination.

To begin to be aware of what I am doing, saying, and thinking is to begin to resist the invasion by my surroundings and by all of my wrong perceptions.

Bring my own inner peaccful countenance to people/turmoil or remove myself from the situation. I determine my level of peace. It does not come from others or things. Inner peace rather than outer peace is desirable.

External peace cannot be developed without internal peace.

Negative memories clutter the mind and take up space needed to imagine a bright future, a new reality.

Have the courage to purify myself of whatever is holding me back.

Do not waste a day of my life waiting for happiness to *find* me.

Adventure is a result of my willingness to live life with a spirit of enthusiasm.

An adventure is any experience that takes me beyond my comfort level to expand and grow.

Security is a state of mind, from knowing I have the power to produce.

> *Worrying does not empty tomorrow of its*
> *troubles; it empties today of its strength.*
> —Mary Engelbreit

Right now, this is how it is. I can either accept it or make myself miserable through resistance.

Consciously focus on the good aspects of my choices rather than the what-ifs.

Don't think too much. I will create a problem that wasn't even there in the first place.

I can get a lot done in life if I do not worry about who gets the credit.

WISDOMS and AFFIRMATIONS

For our present troubles are small and won't last very long.
   —2 Corinthians 4: 17–18 (NLT)

This, too, shall pass.

Sometimes when things are falling apart, they may actually be falling into place.

View crises as interventions that are part of a greater plan—signposts that direct me to my next lesson about my own personal power and sacred contract.

Even when I do not know how help will ever reach me in time, somehow the heavens will move the earth on my behalf … although rarely in the way I expect.

Sense an alert inner stillness in the background while things happen in the foreground.

How I think when I lose determines how long it will be until I win.

By greeting trouble with optimism and hope, I undermine worse troubles down the road.

I am like the blue sky with clouds (pain) blowing past.

The real question is not whether life exists after death. The real question is whether you are alive before death.
   —Osho

Attitude

The tragedy of life is not that I die but what dies inside me when I live.

If I do not enjoy the journey, I probably will not enjoy the destination.

Be sure that I am living my life rather than simply planning my life.

"Yeah, but ..." Never were more fatal words spoken. Yeah, but ... what about debt, my job, my boyfriend, and so forth. "Yeah, but ..." is pernicious (exceedingly harmful, working or spreading in a hidden way). It makes me sound as if I have the best of intentions, when I am really just too scared to do what I should. It allows me to be a coward while sounding noble. "Yeah, but ..." will kill my dreams. Do not squander my time. I will never have it again.

Be a star in my own life. The spotlight is not shining at me—it is radiating from within me.

> *Do not seek for truth; merely cease to cherish opinions.*
> —The Third Zen Patriarch

What am I pretending not to know?

Dependable knowledge harmonizes with natural law and is based on positive thought.

Immerse myself in positive inputs.

Ordinary positive environment is more valuable than getting inspiration from a celebrity.

Truth is not a concept. If I cling to my concepts, I lose reality.

> *Believe those who are seeking truth. Doubt those who find it.*
> —Andre Gide

Is the purpose and goal of life to believe in the truth or to seek it?

Do not seek happiness; it cannot be found. However, freedom from unhappiness is attainable.

My truth will find me, no matter where I hide.

Ignoring the truth only creates more lies and destructive energy.

> *If your lips would keep from slips, five things observe with care: Of whom you speak, to whom you speak, and how and when and where.*
> —Anonymous

Difficult emotions are like disruptive children; they need attention and caring.

Cry when I need to cry; otherwise, the grief will act out in dysfunctional ways later.

Anger expresses the accumulated vehemence of a multitude of minor irritations.

Anger is a signal that something needs to change—quickly.

Attitude

> *The useful and useless must, like good and evil generally,*
> *go on together, and man must make his choice.*
> —Gandhi

God determines who comes into my life. I decide who I let walk away, who I let stay, and who I refuse to let go.

As long as I am not at peace, my behavior carries the energy of my conflict.

Only what I have not given is lacking in any situation.

Only I can evict myself from the garden of paradise.

> *I know nothing except the fact of my ignorance.*
> —Socrates

I am willing to change my attitude about this.

What things of great importance have I learned about others or myself due to this problem?

Whenever I suffer, I must inquire, look at the thoughts I am thinking, and set myself free. I must be a child. Know nothing. Take my ignorance all the way to my freedom.

Calm Yourself

*The world needs you.
It needs your voice, your smile.
It needs your talents, your passion.
It needs all the gifts you have to give.
Listen to your heart, trust your strengths, follow your joy.
Give generously of all those things
That make you so perfectly you.
Because the world needs you
Just as you are.*
—MaryAnne John

All things in nature are not only one with themselves but also one with totality. The deer *is* itself. The flower *is* itself. They do not claim a separate existence from the rest of the universe.

I am precious because I exist; not for anything I *do*.

I am the words to my song.

Calm Yourself

Our deepest fear is not that we are inadequate. Our deepest fear is that we are powerful beyond measure. It is our light, not our darkness that most frightens us. We ask ourselves, "Who am I to be brilliant, gorgeous, talented, and fabulous?" Actually, who are you not to be? You are a child of God. Your playing small does not serve the world. There is nothing enlightened about shrinking so that other people won't feel insecure around you. We are all meant to shine, as children do.

We were born to make manifest the glory of God that is within us. It is not just in some of us; it is in everyone. And as we let our own light shine, we unconsciously give other people the permission to do the same. As we are liberated from our fear, our presence automatically liberates others.
—Marianne Williamson

When I am steadfast in my abstention from harming others (even thoughts such as judgment and jealousy), then all living creatures will cease to feel enmity in my presence.

When I was a child, I was free. I was not afraid to express myself, what I was thinking, what I was feeling. I was like a wild animal. Then I was "domesticated" with belief systems, responsibility, and fears. I was programmed to conform. I began to judge and to be a victim. I became sick with these parasites controlling my brain and thereby controlling me with negative energy. I choose to declare war on the parasite and say *no*! I choose to think positively, become wild again, and be free!

True power develops when, checking impulses and selfishness, one falls back to the higher and calmer consciousness within and to steady oneself upon the unchanging principle of peace, harmony and love that can only be realized by constant meditation, practice, and application.

The more I lose myself in something bigger than myself, the more energy I will have.

> *Life is not as serious as my mind makes it out to be.*
> —*A New Earth* (Eckhart Tolle)

A great deal of time is spent worrying about what the world thinks of us. By the time we reach middle age, we realize that the world was not paying attention while we were worrying.

When someone offers me the gift of their insults and I refuse to accept them, the insult still belongs to the original giver. Therefore, why be upset over something that does not belong to me?

I cannot own what is not mine. I must return the responsibility for others' actions to them.

I do not have to give up my peace just because the world is not going as I would like.

The stream need not think about the river; the river need not think about the ocean. The future will find its own way perfectly.

Eventually all the pieces fall into place. Until then, laugh at the confusion, live for the moment, and know that everything happens for a reason.

Calm Yourself

Man's destiny is to be the trailblazer, to be the first to learn that all creatures have a choice. All creatures are self-aware and intelligent. I can try to thwart the gods and perish trying—or I can stand aside and make room for all the rest to evolve naturally.

> *Calmness is the living breath of God's immortality in you.*
> —Paramahansa Yogananda

Being peaceful is actually God expressing God's self within me.

Remind myself, in moments of strife, that I am first and always a spiritual being, connected to source, and the fruits of good will flow to me and through me.

Act as though I belong to the world, not as if the world belongs to me.

> *Nothing can bring you peace but yourself.*
> —Ralph Waldo Emerson

Worry is just a bad habit, and I can change any habit.

The rough is only mental.

I can choose peace rather than this.

I can elect to be calm by reminding myself that I no longer choose to live in my conditioned past.

There is nothing for me to be upset about.

I have nothing to lose but fear.

Be the harmony and peace I desire.

I *choose* to be happy!

I *choose* peace!

Become a comfortable person.

Joy is vibrantly alive peace.

What is it that stands higher than words? Action. What is it that stands higher than actions? Silence.

Quiet my mind and listen.

Creating a wall of words may blind me to the splendor of the moment.

Only when my noisy mind subsides can I connect with nature at a deep level and go beyond the sense of separation created by excessive thinking.

Peace and God are the same. Being in a peaceful state of grace opens me to spiritual solutions.

The energy of noticing what is right creates excitement to move forward, like plants turning toward the light.

Surround myself with the light of peace; summon peaceful energy toward myself. Imagine a blanket of serenity from God.

Turn to nature, relationships, or a belief in God, seeking strength in my connection to what is unbroken.

Go outside into the sunlight when morbid thoughts overtake me. Light is a faster energy and it will help displace the slower negative energy.

> *To be able to look back upon one's past life*
> *with satisfaction is to live twice.*
> —Martial

Have a mind full of peace, picture peaceful scenes and listen to peaceful sounds, peaceful experiences, and peaceful ideas.

Life is not measured by how many breaths I take but by how many things take my breath away.

> *Once you realize that most people are keeping up appearances*
> *and putting on a show, their approval becomes less important.*
> —J. Peterman

When I know my character is above reproach, what others think is irrelevant.

To free myself from the expectations of others, therein lies self-respect.

People who put me down are not willing to work as hard. They are so busy discouraging everyone else that they lose their edge.

WISDOMS and AFFIRMATIONS

Whatever games are played with us, we
must play no games with ourselves.
—Ralph Waldo Emerson

Removing myself from a negative energy field leaves me uncontaminated and still in a position to remain objective.

Realize that *all* experiences are fleeting and the world (situation, person, place, event) cannot give me anything of lasting value. When the impossible demands of the world are removed, ironically, they become more peaceful.

I am too busy creating beauty to be foolishly engaged in wishing things will improve.

When I think I am happy, am I basing that happiness on surrounding and situations, or on myself as a person.

The peace of God, which surpasses all understanding.
—Philippians 4:7 (ESV)

Good morning, this is God. I will be handling all of your problems today. I will not need your help, so have a miraculous day.

Picture all worry thoughts as flowing out, as I would let water flow from a basin by removing the stopper.

Sometimes surrender means giving up trying to understand and becoming comfortable with not knowing.

In the midst of fighting life's battles, relax.

Calm Yourself

Within every disaster lies the seed of grace.

The universe is conspiring for me in all ways.

> *And I have a feeling that, in the end, probably, training is the answer to a great many things. You can do a lot of things if you're properly trained. And I hope I have been.*
> —Queen Elizabeth II

Work for a cause, not applause. Live life to express, not to impress. Don't strive to make my presence noticed, just to make my absence felt.

Everything is alive and changing all the time, so my *best* will sometimes be high quality and other times not as good. Regardless of the quality, keep doing my best—no more and no less than my best. Trying too hard will spend more energy than needed and, in the end, my best will still not be enough. It will deplete my body and go against myself. Doing less than my best will result in frustration, self-judgment, guilt, and regrets. By doing my best, I will break a big spell that I have been under.

I may not get the brass ring, but I will have a better life.

> *To thine own self be true.*
> —Shakespeare

Truth is found by living truly in my own authentic way.

Vent my frustrations in a controlled yet cleansing manner.

WISDOMS and AFFIRMATIONS

Promise yourself to be so strong that nothing
can disturb your peace of mind.
—Christian Larson

Let all thoughts fall like snowflakes dissolving in the ocean.

To analyze and to remain focused are essential to seeing myself as I really am.

The way to happiness: Keep my mind free from hate. Keep my mind free from worry. Live simply. Expect little. Give much. Fill my life with love. Scatter sunshine. Forget self. Think of others. Do as I would have done to me. See romance in the common place. Have a child's heart. Experience spiritual simplicity.

It is so simple to be happy, yet so difficult to be simple.

Be ye transformed by the renewing of your mind.
—Romans 12:2 (KJV)

What will I do about this? Give me a fresh insight.

Let nothing disturb me. Let nothing frighten me. Everything is temporary.

I am free from fear.

Things are going nicely. Life is good. I choose happiness.

Work hard. Pay your bills on time. Be responsible.
But don't forget to take time for yourself and enjoy life.
—Joe Perepelecta

Calm Yourself

It's good to value the things that money can buy, but it's also good to make sure I haven't lost the precious things in life that money cannot buy.

Live my life. Take chances. Be crazy. Don't wait. Because right now is the oldest I have ever been and the youngest I'll ever be again.

> *You need to associate with people that inspire you, people that challenge you to rise higher, people that make you better. Don't waste your valuable time with people that are not adding to your growth. Your destiny is too important.*
> —Joel Osteen

Don't be someone's downtime, spare time, part time, or sometime. If that person can't be there for me all the time, then he or she is not even worth my time.

There comes a point when I have to realize that I'll never be good enough for some people. The question is, is that my problem or theirs?

God sometimes removes people from my life to protect me. Don't run after them.

Spend less time impressing others and more time impressing myself. Climb a mountain so I can see the world, not so the world can see me.

Do not mistake anonymous with insignificant. God *always* notices, even if no one else does.

WISDOMS and AFFIRMATIONS

Sometimes you've got to be able to listen to yourself and be okay with no one else understanding.
—Christopher Barzak

When I feel alone, keep in mind that aloneness is a temporary place between orbits.

I am in motion to another place, where there will be love and new friends to meet me.

Every experience in life has allowed me to decide what I prefer.

I focus on how I felt when the experiences that I enjoyed occurred.

I have had a variety of experiences to know the difference.

I do not give energy to what was unpleasant.

I aim to be happy.

Gratefulness

*Gratitude is not only the greatest of virtues,
but the parent of all others.*
—Cicero

Happiness will never come to me if I do not appreciate what I already have.

Appreciate what I have before time makes me appreciate what I had.

Life is too short for drama and petty things, so laugh hard, love truly, and forgive quickly.

If my message to the Universe is "gimmee," then the universe will demand of me in return.

I will get back from the world precisely what I gave.

How may I serve? What may I give?

Use my smile to change the world. Don't let the world change my smile.

> *Turn your face to the sun and the shadows fall behind you.*
> —Maori Proverb

Worry never robs tomorrow of its sorrow, but it always robs today of its joy.

Use gratitude and cheerfulness as a measure to test my own spiritual awareness.

Unhappiness is a signal for change.

When I am not happy, it is generally because I am not being truthful with myself.

Integrity creates happiness because it requires me to tell myself the truth about what matters to me.

Where am I hiding or fooling myself?

What one action can I take to bring myself to alignment?

If I want to experience great joy, I need to feel a bit of joy and watch it grow.

Take two minutes at the end of the day for one week to be grateful and notice the effect.

Gratefulness

Happiness depends on the habit of mind we cultivate.
—Norman Vincent Peale

People who push my buttons are my master teachers in developing peace.

Those with lower/slower energies that come into my life are my greatest teachers to remind me that I have yet to master myself in this area. It is a wonderful opportunity to practice transcending this with peace, love, and joy.

Am I finished being miserable?

Everyone will be called to account for all the legitimate pleasures which one failed to enjoy.
—Talmud

This is it—my one and only short life. How shall I live so I enjoy it as much as possible?

How can I make this into a terrific experience?

What are the things that bring a song to my heart, that make me think, *Ah, it is good to be alive?*

Simple pleasures, indulged in frequently, are a key to happiness.

My happiness today will not influence the outcome. I will not feel worse at having rejoiced than if I had not.

Be courageous enough to feel as happy as I can.

Can I choose to be happy in this minute, without a guaranteed future?

Live while I am alive.

I am never going to get this moment back again; therefore, enjoy it.

Each sunrise is a precious jewel, for I am not guaranteed the sunset.

The least things bring the best happiness because the forms of little things only take up a small part of my consciousness, leaving more room for inner space (peace).

> *A human being is not one in pursuit of happiness, but rather in search of a reason to become happy.*
> —Viktor Frankl

Somewhere at the center of life is something unalterably right and good. This *rightness* can be discovered.

Rather than search for the meaning of life, search for the experience of being alive.

Through treasuring my normal days, I create days worth treasuring.

Happiness is the ability to reflect on my life and find it worthwhile—to see it as satisfactory.

Look for the good in life, not the best.

Gratefulness

The highest prize I can receive for creative work is the joy of being creative.

Be happy for no reason, like a child. If you are happy for a reason, you're in trouble, because that reason can be taken from you.
—Deepak Chopra

Sing my own song of happiness, oblivious to how others think I should sing it.

The person who dances must appear insane to the person who cannot hear the music.

Do not ask my mind for permission to enjoy what I do.

Why do I close my eyes when I pray, cry, kiss, or dream? Because the most beautiful things in life are not seen but felt only in the heart.

Joy has no cost.

Success in life is not about things or money. Success is the amount of joy I feel.

To look for substance in material things is to miss most of God's daily gifts to me.

Life brings me everything I need—and more.

Do not moan over the negative things; also, do not cling to the positive things. Simply enjoy it while it is *now*.

Appreciate everything along the path. Drink it all in rather than waiting to get *there*.

The Seven Wonders of the World: To see. To hear. To touch. To taste. To feel. To laugh. To love.

> *I learned how huge he was in my life and how I*
> *had hardly even noticed that fact during his lifetime*
> *because he was so "there". It was like a fish hearing the*
> *word water and not knowing what it means."*
> —*Letting Go of the Person You Used to Be* (Lama Surya Das)

Never become lax in maintaining a state of happiness. Stay afloat on top of it or it will leak away my inner contentment.

When experiencing great delight in watching a beautiful sunset, where does the good feeling go after the sun has set?

This is what I would like to hold on to. Help me memorize this feeling of contentment and help me always support it.

Continuing to pray when the crisis has passed is like sealing the process, helping the soul hold tight to the good attainments.

> *The peace I felt was a closing of accounts and*
> *was connected to the thought of death.*
> —Czeslaw Melosz

Be thankful for the times that force me to be quiet (such as illness), as that gives me the chance to truly listen to my heart.

Gratefulness

In order to experience one thousand joys, I must be willing to touch one thousand sorrows.

> *But I see today that we feel all the freer and lighter for having cast off the tinsel of "civilization."*
> —Gandhi

In trying to enjoy the pleasures of sense, I lose, in the end, my capacity for enjoyment.

Freedom from want is where happiness lives.

Gratitude and appreciation serve me better than attachment and grasping.

> *I am alive, aware, alert, and enthusiastic. I can hardly wait to see what good this day has in store for me. I get up, get going, and keep going. My enthusiasm provides all the energy I need. I move steadily toward greater and greater success in every area of my life. As a child of the infinite, I was born to succeed. I know it, I feel it, I express it, and it is so.*
> —Shelly Severson

My belief at the beginning of a doubtful undertaking is the *one* thing that insures the successful outcome.

I believe I can successfully handle all problems that arise today. I feel good physically, mentally, and emotionally. It is wonderful to be alive. I am grateful for all that I have had, for all that I now have, and for all that I shall have.

Only positive people, experiences, and things come into my life.

I continually improve spiritually, emotionally, physically, intellectually, and financially.

I am full of wonder, delight, acceptance, contentment, and gratitude.

God is now filling my mind with courage, with peace, and with calm assurance. God is now protecting me from all harm. God is now protecting my loved ones from all harm. God is guiding me to the right decisions. God will see me through this situation.

I have the time, energy, health, and finances to be the best me I can be for me.

I am _____. I know it. I desire it. It's on its way. Nothing can stop it. I receive it.

I believe!

> *We can complain because rose bushes have thorns,*
> *or rejoice because thorn bushes have roses.*
> —Abraham Lincoln

Stop focusing on how stressed I am and remember how blessed I am.

If I am incapable of washing dishes joyfully, if I want to finish them quickly so I can go and have a cup of tea, I will be equally incapable of drinking the tea joyfully.

Laughter and irony are at heart reminders that I am not a prisoner in this world but a voyager through it.

Gratefulness

Do not ask to have life's load lifted, but for courage to endure. Do not ask for fulfillment in all your life, but for patience to accept frustration. Do not ask for perfection in all you do, but for wisdom not to repeat mistakes. And finally, do not ask for more before saying "Thank You" for what you have already received.
—Brenda Short

Thank you for keeping me healthy, safe, and prosperous. Thank you for filling me with energy, enthusiasm, joy, wonder, confidence, creativity, and common sense.

Thank you for this glorious body; I treasure it. With Your help, I will begin loving it unconditionally.

I choose to live by choice, not by chance. To be motivated, not manipulated. To be useful, not used. To make changes, not excuses. To excel, not compete. I choose self-esteem, not self-pity. I choose to listen to my inner voice, not to the random opinion of others. I choose to do the things that you won't do so I can continue to do the things you can't.
—Unknown

I receive and accept only good, pure, and lovely people, places, things, and events into my life. Everything else moves away from me to find another accepting recipient.

Three modalities to awakened doing: acceptance, enjoyment, enthusiasm.

Smile in your liver.
—*Eat, Pray, Love* (Elizabeth Gilbert)

Love

Be kind, for everyone you meet is fighting a hard battle.
—Philo

Consider how hard it is to change myself and I will understand what little chance I have in changing others.

Respect the rights of others to be happy.

If you could read the secret history of our enemies, we shall find in each man's sorrow and suffering enough to disarm our hostility.
—Henry Longfellow

To know the needs of men and to bear the burden of their sorrows—that is the true love of men.

Think of what I want and realize that all beings want and need the same things. They are just seeking it through different ways.

Love

I may disapprove of the way someone is going about trying to be happy, but I must remember that we all just want to be happy; their clumsy methods should not disrupt my happiness.

Be a mirror. A mirror does not judge, distort, assume. It merely reflects what is.

> *Sometimes the ones who have the brightest smiles are the ones who have known and endured deep darkness.*
> —Dobinsky

May my broken-heartedness open my heart even further, bringing forth love and open-hearted compassion.

Send love to and pray for my enemies.

Forgiveness means letting go of the hope for a better past.

> *We live happily indeed, not hating those who hate us. Among men who hate us, we dwell free from hatred.*
> —Buddha

When I hated me, I hated you. If I hate someone, I am mistaking that person for me.

My enemy is really my teacher to examine the emotions of anger and revenge and to transcend them.

Anger, hatred, and disharmony are invitations to surrender and love.

Can I love in the face of anger and disrespect?

Why do I allow fear to keep me from others' hearts?

I shall allow no man to belittle my soul by making me hate him.
 —Booker T. Washington

Do not take hatred personally. People are only projecting their feelings of not being loved. Hate cannot penetrate into my soul, which is full of love.

In the face of hatred, stay committed to thoughts of love.

Where there is hatred, let me sow love.
 —Saint Francis

Reciting this prayer in the midst of hatred will shift my thoughts to love.

Love dissolves negativity as light dissolves darkness.

Light equals purity, morality, truth, and clarity.

Putting thoughts of loving white light around someone to help and protect that person is visualizing it being sent by me to do the work of the spirit.

Divine love will meet every human need. Divine love is what I radiate outward.

I must be willing to let divine love solve the problem (allow myself to be the instrument).

Practice allowing the other person to believe that he or she is right.

Love

Practice building up the egos of other people.

> *The meaning of life is to find your gift, and the purpose of life is to give it away.*
> —Pablo Picasso

> *When you meet anyone, remember it is a holy encounter. As you see him, you will see yourself. As you treat him, you will treat yourself. As you think of him, you will think of yourself. Never forget this, for in him you will find yourself or lose yourself.*
> —A Course in Miracles

I only get to keep what I give away.

What I mentally refuse to permit others, I refuse myself. What I bless in others, I draw to myself.

What I refuse to celebrate in your life is what I will not be able to draw into mine.

What I give to others, I give to myself. What I withhold from others, I withhold from myself.

I want people to be happier after I come into a room than before.

Be a delivery person of peace.

Become a peacemaker. Look for opportunities to help.

If possible, help others. If that is not possible, then do no harm to them.

Service without humility is selfishness and egotism.
—Gandhi

Every action, thought, or word I choose to give to someone is ultimately based on how willing I am to share my body, mind, or spirit. I probably will not be generous if I feel threatened in any way, thinking that I will have less if I give some away—or worse, that they will have more.

Let the blessings flow *through* me, not to me.

I am the instrument through which grace flows.

Accept life as a great gift and a great good, not because of what it gives me but because of what it enables me to give others.

Higher awareness is the consciousness of self and others without possessiveness or malice.

All happiness in the world comes from thinking about others, and all the suffering comes from the preoccupation with yourself.
—Shantideva

Make an exhaustive list of everything I could possibly admire about each person who annoys me.

When in grief, it is a good idea to do a thirty-day prayer vigil for the person or event that caused the grief.

The most useful asset of a person is not a head full of knowledge but a heart full of love, with ears open to listen and hands willing to help.

Love

> *Never give up on someone you cannot go
> a day without thinking about.*
> —Levi Bellemore

At every opportunity, tell the people I love that I love them. Forgive those who make me cry. I might not get a second chance.

Every act of love is in some way a promise to forgive. I live on because I can love, and I love because I can forgive.

A good relationship is a birthing process—often painful, often messy.

> *We are all a little weird and life's a little weird, and when we find someone whose weirdness is compatible with ours, we join up with them and fall in mutual weirdness and call it love.*
> —Dr. Seuss

A life lived for one's self alone is not liberation but merely another form of bondage. The highest identity is my relationship with others.

Like two wings that enable a bird to fly, love and wisdom are interdependent.

> *Win her love, earn her respect[,] and keep her trust.*
> —*Shantaram* (Gregory David Roberts)

A long-term romance is like a rose bush. The stem is the friendship, the blossom is the romance, water is the love (the nourishment). The blossom cannot survive without the stem providing the nourishment. In any given season, some blossoms may fall off, but if the bush is well nourished, new blossoms will appear.

Love is a commitment based on one's promise. Feelings rise and fall; commitment stays the same. Commitment is not based on circumstances but on how good my vow is.

The bond of marriage is a good investment only when the interest is kept up.

> *What is the point of being in a relationship with you if it does not motivate me to try to please you, to make your life more pleasurable, to sweeten things for you?*
> —*A Return to Love* (Marianne Williamson)

Marriage is not what I can get out of it but what my husband can get out of it.

Friendship is not about the people I've known the longest. It's about who walked into my life and said, "I'm here for you," then proved it.

Love enough to still want him or her in your life even after seeing what a mess they can be, how moody they can get, and how hard they can be to handle.

The only people I need in my life are the ones who need me in theirs, even when I have nothing to offer but myself.

How beautiful it is to find someone who asks for nothing but your company.

Love

A friend is someone whose presence inspires and elevates me to be the best I can be.

Dive in with both feet; roll up my sleeves and get messy. Dare to live, dare to love, dare to connect.

> *How can I make your day legendary?*
> —Mara

One basic trait toward getting people to like me is to have a sincere and forthright interest in and love for people.

Telling someone that he or she is appreciated is one of the simplest and most incredible things you can ever say.

> *Do I want him to be at peace or do I want him to call?*
> —*A Return to Love* (Marianne Williamson)

Love is the condition in which the happiness of another person is essential to my own.

Is the thing I am angry about more important than the relationship?

I am not held back by the love I did not receive in the past but by the love I am not extending in the present.

> *Show respect even to people who don't deserve it; not as a reflection of their character, but as a reflection of yours.*
> —Dave Willis

Overlook (forgive) the unconsciousness (ego) in others.

Hold no one or nothing in judgment. In the world of spirit, there is no right or wrong.

My task is to infuse my actions with all my faith and belief in its goodness and release it into the universe to do its invisible work (as well as detach from the outcome).

What you react to in another, you strengthen in yourself.
—*A New Earth* (Eckhart Tolle)

To the extent I perceive your guilt or innocence, I am bound to perceive my own.

When I affirm someone's innocence or fortify his or her guilt, it is how I feel about myself.

Do onto others as I would have them do unto me, for even if they don't, I will feel as though they did.

Forgiveness allows me to be cleansed and helps ease my pain.

Forgiveness is like unlocking the door to set someone free and realizing that I was the prisoner.

Who am I truly hurting?

They know not what they do.
—Luke 23:34 (KJV)

Holding on to anger is like drinking poison and expecting the other person to die.
—Buddha

Love

How can I live a productive life and all that goes with it if I am controlled by hate?

Hate, like cancer, if not dealt with, kills one day at a time.

Guilt is the hilt of the knife I use on myself, and love is the blade; worry keeps it sharp.

> *Love and do what you will.*
> —Saint Augustine

Love is not neutral. It takes a stand. It is a commitment to the attainment of the conditions of peace for everyone involved in a situation.

I invite the highest good for all concerned to be here now.

Dear guardian angels: Please bring options this day for my highest good and commune with the guardian angels of others to bring us all options, meetings, and synchronicities for our highest good and in divine perfection.

Sometimes I love with nothing more than hope. Sometimes I cry with everything but tears.

> *Whatever you decide to do, make sure it makes you happy.*
> —Paulo Coelho

I have to like who I am before I am who I like.

Invest in something that cannot lose; invest in myself.

People who love themselves don't treat themselves poorly.

Talk aloud to myself. Work up a superiority complex. Look in the mirror and build pride in myself.

Accept the love I think I deserve.

> *The greatest gifts you can give your children are the roots of responsibility and the wings of independence.*
> —Denis Waitley

Enlightened people don't ask anyone to believe anything. They simply point the way and leave it to the people to realize it for themselves.

I cannot save everyone. No matter how much I try to help them, some people are going to destroy themselves.

I can only help you so far.

> *Why does modern biology accept only competition to be the fundamental operating principle and only aggression to be the fundamental trail of living beings? Why does it reject cooperation as an operating principle and why does it not see altruism and compassion as possible traits for the development of living beings as well?*
> —Dhali Llama

> *The idea of "survival of the fittest" has been misused to condone and in some cases justify excess human greed and individualism and to ignore ethical models for relating to our fellow human being in a more compassionate spirit.*
> —Dhali Llama

It is only now that we are able to destroy ourselves that we understand the ultimate cause and effect of not living in harmony.

The most important lesson I have to learn is that a society that does not live in harmony is bound to destroy itself.

Unity and cooperation offer a greater chance of survival than can ever be realized from competition and conflict.

> *Cooperativeness is not so much learning how to get along with others as taking the kinks out of ourselves, so that others can get along with us.*
> —Thomas S. Monson

Ask myself what is important to make visible what I am fighting about. Ask the other person the same question to find common ground.

Lack of communication starts with a fear of how the other will react. If it is worth thinking about, it is worth talking about. Avoid the anger, criticism, and complaining, not the topic.

Compromise—at least enough to make things better.

How much do I love another? Enough to tell the truth about myself?

Truly strong people share their weaknesses.

Do not look at me; look beyond me.

Other people care less about my thinking or about me and more about what I think about them.

The grinding poverty and starvation with which our country is afflicted is such that it drives more and more men every year into the ranks of the beggars, whose desperate struggle for bread renders them insensible to all feelings of decency and self-respect. And our philanthropists, instead of providing work for them and insisting on their working for bread, give them alms.
—Gandhi

Civility is the most difficult part of Satyagraha [insistence on truth]. *Civility does not here mean the mere outward gentleness of speech cultivated for the occasion, but an inborn gentleness and desire to do the opponent good. These should show themselves in every act of a Satyagraha. ... The end of a Satyagraha campaign can be described as worthy, only when it leaves the Satyagrahis stronger* [that is, with stronger self-worth plus more respect for the opponent] *and more spirited than they are in the beginning.*
—Gandhi

There is no alternative to compassion; recognizing human value and the oneness of humanity is the only way to achieve lasting happiness.

Love

As we cut our ties with our ancestors[,] we find ourselves helpless in a world of dizzying change, cut off from memory and forethought. Without context, information becomes meaningless; without perspective, events cannot be evaluated; without connections in time and space, we are lonely and lost.... Rituals are a public affirmation of meaning, value, connection. They tie people to each other, to their ancestors and to their place in the world together.
—David Suzuki

A child's life is like a piece of paper on which every passer-by leaves a mark.
—Chinese Proverb

Whatever is true, whatever is noble, whatever is right, whatever is pure, whatever is lovely, whatever is admirable—if anything is excellent or praiseworthy—think about such things.
—Philippians 4:8 (NIV)

Thought impregnated with love becomes invincible.

When I feel hatred and aversion, I must contemplate love and understanding. In this way, I will become more balanced and my mind becomes more settled.

Be all the things (kindness, compassion, and generosity) that I want to show up in my life and be those things to myself first.

Show me what love is.

Ego

Complaining is one of ego's favorite strategies for strengthening itself.
—*A New Earth* (Eckhart Tolle)

The ego needs problems to strengthen its identity.

Egos need conflict, us against them, a victim mentality, any form of comparison. It is addicted to unhappiness. Therefore, it cannot tolerate happiness for very long.

Ego thinking: If they are *wrong*, then I am *right* and therefore superior.

Suffering begins when I mentally name or label a situation in some way as bad or undesirable. Little stories in the form of complaints feed the ego's need for drama (What a miserable day. It's is raining. He did not call. She let me down. I was there; she was not.)

When circumstances are not good and I do not feel happy, my gremlin (ego) will do everything possible to make it last as long as possible. It will encourage me to focus on the unpleasant circumstances. It will make mountains out of molehills and encourage me to spend time in my head considering the ins and outs of the external situation, in the futile attempt of making myself right, wrong, plotting revenge, or justifying my action. It wants me to waste my time preserving a concept. It will convince me that preserving my concept and habit is the same as preserving my life.

My actual enemy (fear) is my selfish attitude within myself, my self-grasping attitude, and my distorted views.

My ego is the embodiment of my own self-hatred.

> *Wanting keeps the ego alive more than having.*
> —*A New Earth* (Eckhart Tolle)

The ego, left unchecked, always wants more; and like a cancer, will eventually destroy the host (me).

Who would I be if I gave up my problems?

The fault in others may only be perceived by my mind, which has been conditioned to see wrongdoing by my ego's past.

Eliminate the ego's need to make someone wrong.

It is hard enough trying to clean up my own act. Trying to clean up someone else's is just an ego trick to keep me from applying myself to my own lessons.

Adversity introduces me to myself.

Imagine accusations as loosening the chains of my own self-cherishing.

> *They are forever free who renounce all selfish desires and break away from the ego-cage of I, me, and mine to be united with the Lord. This is the supreme state.*
> *Attain to this and pass from death to immortality.*
> —Sri Krishna

Attempting to feel spiritual erects a barrier by introducing ego into the picture.

Ego wants to explain, defend, and monitor how spiritual I am, counting spiritual points.

Defending/arguing about my faith is to move into an area of ego—needing to be right; therefore, away from spirit.

When I stumble in my faith, it is because I am self-consumed.

Awareness and ego cannot coexist—like light and dark. The moment I become aware of the ego, it is weakened.

When my ego becomes lonely, upset, fearful, frustrated (which it does in order to confirm the lower value it places on life), my spirit must transcend ego. Remember that I am connected to the source that keeps my heart beating.

The light, the thought that I might indeed be good enough, is such a threat to the ego that it takes out its biggest guns to defend against it. For example, meanness and bullying are just armor against the light.

Am I willing to let go of the payoff of ego? Am I willing to love God more than ego? Am I willing to let go of willfulness?

Get ego out of the way. Trust the source!

> *You can value or care for things, but whenever you get attached to them, you will know it is the ego.*
> —*A New Earth* (Eckhart Tolle)

The central act of ignorance is false identification (that is, I am *not* my work, my body, my title, or my achievements). I am *not* my ego.

Abstaining from falsehood (confusing my identity with the ego world of possessions and achievements) will transfer to everything and everyone surrounding me.

When a situation switches from pleasure to pain, reflect on the fact that the deeper nature of the original pleasure reveals itself.

Attachment to such superficial pleasures will only bring more pain.

The most consistently troublesome thing about loss is the destruction of expectations.

> *Has who I am become diminished* [by the loss of any material thing]?
> —*A New Earth* (Eckhart Tolle)

Becoming upset or anxious at the threat of loss means my ego is attached to it.

The quest for wealth is like a vain pursuit of a mirage.

The meaning in *things* is how much I use them to contribute to the world. If perceived lovingly, they can lift the vibrational energy in the world around me. For example, clothes and make-up are a form of art and beauty—or vanity.

If I cling to nothing, I can handle anything.

Being does not have *self*. It just *is*.

Infinite

For I know the thoughts and plans that I have for you, says the Lord, thoughts and plans for welfare and peace and not for evil, to give you hope in your final outcome.
—Jeremiah 29:11 (AMPC)

I am turning this over to the invisible force that digests my food and circulates my blood, while always keeping in mind that I am connected at all times to that source.

I will trust in the same power that moves galaxies and creates babies rather than in my own self-indulgent assessments of how I would like thing to go.

You don't have a soul. You are a soul. You have a body.
—C. S. Lewis

I am a spirit being having a human experience.

Trust the perfection that resides within me.

Practice the presence of spirit.

> *Do you not know that you are the temple of God*
> *and the spirit of God dwells in you?*
> —1 Corinthians 3:16 (NAS)

I am not flawed. I am a piece of the divine God—flawless.

In the midst of disharmony, reminding myself to abstain from the false identity with the material world will bring me back to my true essence.

Reminding myself that I am united with God in the very instant of strife will allow my thoughts and affirmations to become my reality.

> *God is love, and the one who abides in love*
> *abides in God, and God abides in him.*
> —1 John 4:16 (NASB)

I am divinely connected to God and to all of God's creations.

Life can change form, but it cannot be destroyed. My spirit is inseparable from the Infinite.

Spirituality is from within, the result of recognition (the availability of an invisible force), realization (of its presence), and reverence (by quietly communing with it).

Rather than asking an external god to solve my problems for me, identify myself as part of the beloved divine creation that I am.

Recognizing myself as a child of the most high, as a divine presence, will facilitate rising and maintaining that higher, faster spiritual energy field. And it is from this new energy field that I bring sparks of the divinity that nullify and eradicate those problems in my life.

> *Your eyes are too pure to look on evil; you*
> *cannot tolerate wrongdoing.*
> —Habakkuk 1:13 (NIV)

When I live in the world of spirit, I remember that God made everything and that it is all good. What is not good is not of God, but only in my mind and not real.

God is only about good, God is everywhere, and God made everything; therefore, problems are illusions. God is too pure to behold iniquity. God made all that was made, and all that God made was good. My eyes are too pure to look at evil. I cannot tolerate wrong.

Non-good is an illusion that disappears when spirit is present.

If I ask God to heal me, I am saying God made me sick.

God is good, God is the creator, God is omnipresent, and all that is non-God cannot exist, except if I allow it in my thoughts.

WISDOMS and AFFIRMATIONS

*If we come from unlimited abundance, then
we must be what we came from.*
—Wayne Dyer

God dwells within me—as me.

To deny God within myself is to deny God everywhere.

My hand responds to the directives of my mind. My organs act in accordance with the central divine intelligence within them. Remind my body to perform as it was created to perform. Direct, insist, and demand my mind to be in harmony with the divine mind.

Mortal sense needs to yield to make room for spiritual awareness.

God finds ways of expressing His power in ways I can accept. Giving up my limited understanding of the world is more of a threat than the broken leg (that is, I can accept a doctor and a cast but not an instant mending).

When I come to believe I am separate from God, my mind tells me that I have a problem; but I am *never* separate from God!

Yield to the one to whom all things owe their existence.

Infinite forces were here before I was and will continue beyond the boundaries of death and time.

My son,... you are always with me, and everything I have is yours.
—Luke 15:31 (NIV)

God is not withholding. Stop asking God to give what I think He is withholding. Instead, I can bring this spirit of God that dwells in me to those things missing or problem areas. Then I will have unlocked the secret for spiritual solutions to my problems.

I cannot influence God. God does not hoard everything, make me beg and ask in a certain way, then decide if I am worthy of receiving, while delighting in watching me suffer.

God has no ego by which to be insulated if I do not get His name right.

I am not being punished.

Instead of asking favors, bring the loving presence of God to the situation.

God is not hidden from me. I can commune with this omnipresent source and bring love to bear on personal problems.

Do not be anxious about anything, but in everything by prayer and supplication with thanksgiving let your requests be known unto God. And the peace of God, which surpasses all understanding, will guard your hearts and your minds (thoughts) *in Christ Jesus.*
—Philippians 4:6-7 (ESV)

Go to the abundant ocean of blessing many times with a bucket, not only once with a thimble.

Everything that I consider to be missing from my life stems from my failure to understand and apply God's laws of abundance.

Pray to be in God consciousness, where thoughts of scarcity dissolve. Feel directed to attract the missing pieces of my life like iron filings to a magnet.

> *And the truth will set you free.*
> —John 8:32 (NIV)

If I accept God as the truth, then I must accept love as the truth and that evil is false.

Think of all good as God expressing Himself and evil/wrong/discord as ignorance of this truth.

Evil first exists as a thought of non-good or non-God. Correct that error in thinking and the non-good will disappear as quickly as two plus two equals seven.

> *All you have to do is awaken from the belief in two powers of good and evil and begin to honor God by respecting the first commandment ... How can you fear an evil power if there is only one power and that one power is God?*
> —Joel Goldsmith

God cannot be divided against God.

God is not an overcoming power. Since God is the *only* power, there is no secondary power to subdue.

Give up my belief in a second power.

By believing in two powers (good versus evil), I must constantly upgrade my fighting to defeat the weaker force.

Infinite

"Resist not evil" (Matthew 5:39) (KJV) means giving up fighting my problems. Avoid giving any power, in my mind or daily life, to the presence of problems. When I become a fighter against anything, I join forces with that which created it, in the form of a counterforce.

"Resist not evil" (Matthew 5:39) (KJV) means do not give credence to evil as a power in the first place.

Harmony is my normal, natural state of being. If my mind believes in two powers, it is possible to create disharmony for myself. (For example, if I think I will get a flat tire when I am in a hurry, I probably will.) Being in a natural state of harmony (in tune with God), I am no longer limited by the boundaries of mind and body. I will reap the fruits of synchronicity wherein I work together with fate to manage the coincidences of my life.

I will now bring the one power of good to these thoughts of anguish, and they will be nullified.

> *God saw all that He had made, and behold, it*
> *was very good.* (God created *everything*).
> —Genesis 1:31 (NASB)

If it is not good, it is not of God; and if it is not of God, it cannot exist, since everything is of the one power I call God.

Problems cannot survive in the presence of God.

Problems disappear; love remains.

Perfect love casts out fear.
—1 John 4:18 (NASB)

Fear represents a disbelief in God at that moment.

Fearing (not believing in or avoiding my divinity) can become commonplace.

Would I ever fear if I knew (without a doubt) that God was my real self?

I cannot have God and have fear too.

Fear and love cannot exist at the same time.

Fear cannot exist where God is (and vice versa).

With God all things are possible.
—Matthew 19:26 (NIV)

Does that exclude anything?

If God be for us, who can be against us?
—Romans 8:31 (KJV)

When I *know* who walks beside me, how can I doubt?

In the midst of problems, anxiety, and so forth, stop and remember the presence of God.

The power of God is creative and sustaining.

Infinite

Be still, and know that I am God.
—Psalm 46:10 (NIV)

Stillness is the language God speaks; everything else is a bad translation.

Stillness is the only thing in this world that has no form.

Because thoughts come out of stillness, they have power to take me back into the same stillness from which they arose. That stillness is also inner peace, and that stillness and peace are the essence of my being.

I must slow down to speed up my spiritual energy. In the world of physical form, the actual energy pattern is very slow. Light and spirit vibrate very fast. Slow down, meditate on peace and spirit, and vibrate faster.

I must be able to radiate outward that which I am inside—a divine, peaceful being.

Do not feel spiritual—be it!

Satori is the arising of inner spaciousness where before there was a clutter of thoughts and turmoil of emotion.

Ananda equates to the bliss of being.

When we pray to God we must be seeking nothing—nothing.
—Saint Francis

Do not pray asking for *things,* but pray to keep my connection to God.

Asking for things is putting the material world above the spiritual.

Fear of not having enough reveals a lack of faith in the invisible power that supports me.

The presence of fear is a sure sign that I trust my own strength, not God's.

Prayer is spiritual energy.

God only has the power that I give Him.

God does His part when I do mine.

> *Where you fall, there your God pushed you down.*
> —Nigerian proverb

When God wants to educate me, He does not send me to the school of graces but to the school of necessities.

Many crises in my life are divinely scheduled to get me to go in another direction. No one wants to get off a comfortable couch.

I will not find peace by rearranging the circumstances of my life.

Heaven gives me chances to break free from past choices and consequences, to transcend the fog of past programming. The mind will throw up objections, but I must listen to intuition.

When God takes something from my grasp, He is not punishing me but merely opening my hands to receive something better.

Have the courage to purify myself of whatever may be holding me back.

> *Faith is the bird that sings when the dawn is still dark.*
> —Tagore

Faith (trust in the unknown) is like an invisible and invincible magnet that attracts what it desires and expects.

Approach life with a sense of possibility rather than foreboding or helplessness.

Look for affirmation that growth and restoration are possible.

Faith dares me to imagine what I might be capable of. It enables me to reach for what I do not yet know with a measure of courage.

Faith gives me resilience in time of difficulty and the ability to respond to challenges without feeling trapped.

Faith teaches me that whatever disappointments I might meet, I can try again, trust again, and love again.

> *We all dance to a mysterious tune, intoned in the distance by an invisible piper.*
> —Albert Einstein

The Bible is the sheet music. My life is the melody.

God experiences life through me.

> *When you are aware that you are thinking, that awareness is not part of thinking. It is a different dimension of consciousness. And it is that awareness that says 'I Am'.*
> —*A New Earth* (Eckhart Tolle)

"I am bored, angry, and afraid." Who knows this? I am the knowing, not the condition that is known.

If I can become comfortable with not knowing who I am, then what is left is who I am—the being side of human, pure potential versus already defined.

Think like God. *I am that I am.*

> *Religion is an offense against a religious experience.*
> —Jung

There is nothing wrong with religion or science but with what I think they are—how I interpret them.

Science studies the world I live in; religion studies sacred books that hold the secrets about the world I live in.

Sometimes divine revelation simply means adjusting my brain to hear what my heart already knows.

Infinite

A ritual is like a clue, a road map. It is an enactment of a myth. By participating in a solid ritual, you are actually experiencing a mythological life. It's out of that one can learn to live spiritually. A mythological life is a spiritual life.
—Joseph Campbell

All philosophies and religions have safeguarded important ideas that help to understand ourselves and the forces that govern the universe (God).

What rituals lift my spirits? What diminishes my spirits?

My life is a pathway of awakening.

"Not all at once can the soul talk to God, be He ever so near. If the heavenly language never has been learned, quick as is the spirit sense in seizing the facts it needs, then the poor soul must use the words and phrases it has lived on and grown into day by day."
—*Rebecca of Sunnybrook Farm* (Kate Douglas Wiggin)

Lord, I can't offer you much in the way of a partnership, but please join with me and help me. I don't know how You can help me, but I want to be helped. So I now put my business, myself, my family, and my future in Your hands. I am ready to hear and follow Your advice if You will make it clear.

According to your faith be it onto you.
—Matthew 9:29 (KJV)

Do not let fear carry more authority than faith.

Solutions are attributes to my immersion in the world of spirit.

I receive the expanding receptive forward movement of the infinite mind of intention.

If you have faith ... nothing shall be impossible unto you.
—Matthew 17:20 (AKJV)

Performing miracles is not a matter of doing the impossible; it is a matter of redefining the possible.

Doubt is the result of want or weakness of faith.

Problems represent a deficit of spirit.

Practice being aware of the impossibility of being outside the omnipresent spirit.

God's gifts are given as freely as the air and the sunshine.
—Ernest Holmes

All miracles are really the same magnitude; it is all God's grace.

The source of all energy—energy in the sun, in the atom, in the flesh, in the bloodstream, in the mind. I hereby draw energy from this illimitable source.

Until one is committed, there is hesitancy, the chance to draw back, always ineffectiveness. Concerning all acts of initiation (and creation) ... the moment one definitely commits oneself, then Providence moves too. All sorts of things occur to help one that would never otherwise have occurred.
—William Hutchison Murray

Infinite

The universe paces my empowerment to the speed of my willingness to act on my empowerment.

The more I know God, the more normal I become, and I begin to fulfill the purpose of my life.

Trust the journey, even when I don't understand it.

> *Oh, Son of Spirit, love me that I may love thee. If thou lovest me not, my love can in no way reach thee. Know this, O servant.*
> —Seen on the Camino de Santiago

My true identity is the mind of the mind, the eye of the eye, the breath of the breath—the finding of God.

I ask that the love that surrounds me and connects me to everyone and everything please guide me right now.

Meditation

The goal is the path, the way of enlightened living.

Indra's Jeweled Net: *At each knot is a crystal gem, which is connected to all the other gems and reflects in itself all others. On such a net, no gem is in the centre or at the edge. Each and every jewel is at the centre in that it reflects all the other jewels on the net. At the same time, it is the edge in that it is itself reflected in all other jewels.*
—Dhali Llama

When observing subatomic phenomena, it is impossible to separate completely the observer from what is being observed. In fact, there are really no objects in the world at all, only vibrations of energy and relationships.

May I attain highest enlightenment for the sake of all beings.

Love of life in all its forms is a by-product of spiritual development.

Meditation

I shall lead a life of moral principles and not engage in anything that brings harm to others, even if I cannot help them.

> *In hearing, there is just hearing, no hearer and nothing heard.*
> *In seeing, there is just seeing, no seer and nothing seen.*
> —Buddha

Who were you and what did you look like before your parents were born?

I am being pulled to my destiny, not from my past.

I am not my thoughts, emotions, sense perceptions, and experiences. I am not the content of my life. I am the space in which all things happen.

I am not the *thinker*; I am the one who is aware of the thinking.

> *Each of us is a God. Each of us knows all.*
> *We need only open our minds to hear our own wisdom.*
> —Buddha

Daily meditation is mental hygiene, a form of mental floss that retards truth decay.

By practicing meditation, I carry within my own heart a portable paradise.

Meditation is not the means to the end. It is both the means and the end.

Everything changes through cause and effect. Emotions can be seen as a field of forces, in which opposing mental states (anger and hostility versus love and compassion) interact in constant dynamic, making me either weak or strong. If I meditate on the right conditions, I can consciously direct a change of the state of my mind, transforming my thoughts and emotions positively thus changing my life. However, as it takes time to heat a cold room, the process is gradual.

Karma implies that everything I say, think, or do has an effect. My conditioning and repetition will be my destiny. When I change, my future changes.

The *Om Namah Shivaya* mantra or chant consists of six syllables: *om*, *na*, *mah*, *shi*, *va*, *ya*. When chanted properly, each syllable activates certain energy centers within my body as I meditate upon the energy of Lord Shiva. Shiva is often referred to as the part of the Hindu trinity, which has dominion over death and destruction. *Om*, or *aum*, is the pranava, or seed mantrapranava, of all mantras. The two syllables *na* and *mah* can be translated as "I humbly bow to you." The three syllables *shi*, *va*, and *ya* invoke Lord Shiva and all his energies to bless me and lead me to the highest state of peace and meditation. (death to problems)

Soham or *Hamsa* is sometimes called the *so hum* breath. They are actually the same mantra. The syllables are reversed according to whether one inhales or exhales first. According to the grammar of the Sanskrit language, when the syllables are reversed, *so* becomes *sa*. Soham is a mantra affirming *I am that I am*, a powerful mantra. In meditation, mentally repeat this mantra to harmonize with the breath.

Meditation

Breathing in, I am aware of my heart. Breathing out, I smile to my heart.

With each exhalation, let go a little more. Die a little with each exhalation. Let go of things, plans, people, emotions, ideas, fears, opinions.

Feel the life that animates my body.

The way is not difficult for those who have no preferences.

Your vision will become clear only when you look into your heart. Who looks outside, dreams. Who looks inside, awakens.
—Carl Jung

The more I deprive my senses, the more I perceive and create. That is why I meditate.

Eat little. Sleep little. Speak little. Whatever is a worldly habit, lessen it; go against its power. This is called discipline. It causes the mind to become dissatisfied and it struggles. It experiences suffering. Only then will I know how to practice meditation.

Dullness, boredom, restlessness, and agitation are also forms of suffering.

Stirring up my outer world is a way to deal with inner dissatisfaction.

Long and seemingly pointless work projects help to frustrate my attachment to tranquility. Monotonous jobs help to emphasize the need to surrender to the way things are and to stress the observance of the Vinaya (discipline).

When I practice samadhi (intense concentration) I want peace and tranquility, but I do not get any because I have never practiced this way. When tranquility does not come in a short time, I suffer and then quit trying. I have no discipline.

This is practice/discipline. If I feel like doing it, I do it. If I do not feel like doing it, I do it anyway. I just keep doing it. Eventually, it will all come together, bringing enlightenment.

The duties of a meditator are mindfulness, collectedness, and contentment.

The essence of discipline is first self-awareness, then self-control.

Non-resistance, non-judgment, and non-attachment are the three aspects of true freedom and enlightened living.

Acceptance, enjoyment, and enthusiasm are the three ways for consciousness to flow into what I do and thus into the world through energy frequencies.

In the sky, there is no distinction of east or west; people create distinctions out of their minds and then believe them to be true.
—Buddha

The dripping tap did not come just to annoy me. It is merely a sound.

Like the sound of a drum, which arises from the interplay between stick beating on a drum skin held together by wood and brackets, it is all like echoes and reflections. Everything is in process.

Meditation

There is nothing concrete or real behind the sound—or behind anything. It is all like magic and so marvelous.

When I accept the way things are and accept the true nature of things, I can let go; my outlook changes and I become more peaceful. Thinking and feeling will still be there but will be deprived of power. I will not longer pout, like an annoying child, why I have not yet become enlightened.

As oil and water can share the same bottle but still be separate, so can my heart and thoughts versus my feelings.

The mind is similar to a leaf. When there is no wind, it remains still, but when a breeze of mental impression blows, it flaps and flutters; the natural state of the mind is stillness, clean and clear (like water).

As a horse or dog must be trained before it can be useful for work and its strength of benefit to me, in the same way, my mind must be trained to bring blessings and benefit to me.

Negative thoughts are like small children who do not know any better. Teach them the power of positive thoughts.

I see new paths and options. I am filling up with courage and confidence. I trust myself to make good choices and decisions and to create a good future for myself. I know that when I feel this way, my thoughts and feelings are positive and draw good things to me.

I release any energy I do not want. I send it out into the universe to be transformed into light. I call back to myself any of my energy I have left scattered out in the universe.

$E=mc^2$: Energy (my level of awareness) is mass (my desire) coming at me faster than the speed of light.

As I become aware of what I do not want, my desire about what I do want comes into clearer focus. Refocusing my awareness to what I do want refocuses my energy and my emotional set point to a higher level, thereby channeling the law of attraction.

The law of attraction is like having an efficient manager take care of every detail for me.

The energy is always working. Do I know how to work with the energy?

I give energy to what I think about. My emotions indicate if I am in alignment with source. When feelings of doubt or worry come, I simply shift the thoughts back to how I *will* feel when my desire has manifested. I give thought (energy) back to the positive.

Energy flows where attention goes.

Accept that the stream of well-being that flows to me from the non-physical is never ending. And in that remembered knowing, I will once again be in vibrational harmony. When I am in vibrational harmony only with what I want, then only what I want comes.

Meditation

What I am thinking and feeling creates a vibrational pattern, and it radiates out from me and magnetizes to me energy, situations, and people who are in vibrational harmony with my vibrational pattern. When I change my thoughts and change my energy (my vibrations), I change my world.

To observe ghosts of the past deeply, to recognize their nature and transform them, is to transform the past. They are my internal patterns that are sometimes quietly asleep, while at other times, they awaken suddenly and act in a strong way.

To have my spirit spread out across ten years of history (reliving the past), still processing experiences that are old, drains my life force. The more psychic weight I have, the longer I have to wait for things to happen in my life—like spontaneous assistance.

> *Just as it is known that an image of one's face is seen dependent on a mirror but does not really exist as a face, so the conception of "I" exists dependent on mind and body, but like the image of a face, the "I" does not at all exist as its own reality.*
> —Nagarjuna's Precious Garland of Advice

When *this* is, *that* arises (short only exists when there is long). They do not exist through their own natures. Due to the production of *this*, *that* is produced, like light from the production of a flame.

Inherent existence does not exist! Phenomena *can* perform functions or act as cause and effect.

WISDOMS and AFFIRMATIONS

*It is not the outer objects that entangle us. It is
the inner clinging that entangles us.*
—Tilopa

Even if nirvana is right here, I am often elsewhere.

When things go wrong, ask myself, "Where is my energy? I need to be fully present, in the now." Then allow the laws of attraction, and cause and effect to pull together a synchronistic response.

Worldly knowledge is really ignorance. It is not knowledge with clear understanding; therefore, there is never an end to it. It revolves around worldly goals of accumulating things, a mass delusion that has me stuck.

When my mind follows my moods, I am like a child with no parents to care for me, an orphan with no refuge, therefore insecure.

When I am too preoccupied with the affairs of this life, I face circumstances that are more adverse. Whereas when I adopt a rational and realistic approach to life, I have less trouble and fewer difficulties.

The past is remembered *now*. The future is thought about *now*.

Do I have a future moment to get to that is more important than now?

When I move my attention into the *now*, there is alertness.

The mind is fickle; do not rely on it.

Meditation

Neither money nor technology can help develop inner peace.

> *Human energy is low and the divine energy is without limit. You are God. You are the divine energy when you do the divine work. Your energy grows.*
> —Sai Baba

My brain is both a receiving set and a broadcasting station for the vibrations of thought.

What are my thoughts at the beginning of my day? What mood do they put me in?

What thoughts are at the end of my day, taking me into my dreams?

What I hold in my awareness, I move toward naturally.

> *If you can recognize illusion as illusion, it dissolves. The recognition of illusion is also its ending. Its survival depends on your mistaking it for reality.*
> —*A New Earth* (Eckhart Tolle)

My physical senses are low vibrational and processed by my mind, which is where the problem is perceived but not real.

When I leave my spiritual consciousness, I create an opening for slower-moving frequencies to enter and large enough for other incompatible lower frequencies to cause damage to many areas of my life.

Put a light around negative thoughts and things I do not want. Imagine them dissolving into the light.

I must attune to the vibrational energy field of God to be able to receive spiritual guidance.

I can create the higher energy to access spiritual solutions at will.

But such is the irresistible nature of truth,
that all it asks, and all it wants, is the liberty of appearing.
—Thomas Payne

Both believers and cynics are more interested in justifying themselves and demonstrating that their ideas are right than in seeking the truth.

In order to achieve liberation, one must develop a strong will to achieve it. It is necessary to identify and reflect on suffering, mainly our suffering of conditioning.

If desire, anger, or dislike arises in my mind, I need to investigate to see how and from where it arose. Contemplate such things and see how they work against me—to understand in a pure mind, with practice, not by only reading and theory.

I must become fed up with both my likes and dislikes, my suffering and my happiness, before I am ready for the true dhamma.

Bad circumstances are assisting in my spiritual development.

Meditation

Getting into a jam and being forced to make a decision summons life force. I cannot get it wrong. Make a decision and let it flow. Going limp and being undecided never gets it done.

Renunciation implies allowing rather than controlling, letting go of holding back.

If I were carrying a heavy rock and someone said "Throw it away," I'd say, "If I throw it away, I will not have anything left." Only when it becomes so heavy that I drop it do I realize the benefit of letting go. Later, I more readily will let it go.

Let go of old ways of thinking and access awareness.

If I am strong and clear about my positive wanting and feeling it, then bad things simply cannot get in. Positive energy and negative energy simply cannot mix with me.

When problems arise or my mind wanders in meditation, I think of such things as obstacles on the road when walking. Go around them and then do not think about them anymore. Also, do not worry about obstacles that I have not seen yet.

> *When something is "out of control[,]" it is*
> *merely out of your control, not God's.*
> —Pastor John Hagee

A problem that appears to have no solution causes too much stress, and people therefore ignore reality (denial).

I have conflicts with other people and with my environment because of an incomplete understanding arising from a bad perception of reality.

Reality is for people who lack imagination.

If I can admit that I do not know everything and open myself to things I do not understand, it is infinite possibility.

Open and relax the tight fist of grasping; infinite space is there—open, inviting, and comfortable.

When my upper chakra works with the compassion of the heart chakra, inspiration, strength, drive, commitment, and faith all rush directly to my lower, biological, survival, friendship and giving chakras.

Om Mani Padme Hung—the jewel is in the lotus. The jewels I desire (wisdom, compassion) are already in me, waiting to unfold.

Slow vibrations result in an ego consciousness, being self-absorbed, being far from God (spirit), and having many problems.

Medium vibrations result in group consciousness, having an us/them mentality, relationship problems (me versus them), having a victim/judgment mentality, having health problems (me versus illness), and financial woes (I don't have but they do).

Fast vibrations result in unity/no separation, having a God consciousness, and being connected to everything/everyone.

Meditation

> *The Tao does nothing, yet leaves nothing undone.*
> —Tao Te Ching

> *Healing does not always mean staying on the side of life.*
> *Sometimes God has other plans for his children—*
> *and both sides of life are really one.*
> —Peace Pilgrim

When death is denied, life loses depth.

> *An absence of belief was required for my healing.*
> —Anita Moorjani

Perception controls genes.

Disease and illness are not real in that they do not exist in the spiritual realm. My body may be sick, but my spirit is not. Therefore, my spirit can heal the body.

Energy cannot be destroyed, but it can be transformed. Hate can turn to love, sickness to health.

> *My magnificence decided it wanted to live, so*
> *every cell in my body responded in kind.*
> —Anita Moorjani

Think of disease and injury in terms of energy. The body is immobilized due to incompatible frequencies of the higher self.

The healing of the human gene pool is about releasing trapped pain and fear by transforming old thought patterns that contain restrictive attitudes and bringing out a higher state of consciousness within the body.

The body resonates with every intuitive hit. To ignore—become deliberately unconscious—the intuition leaves the body upset, which can result in physical illness.

When feeling ill, instead of feeling guilty or weak, remind myself to shift to the realization of being connected to God.

The closer I get to God (vibrate faster), the more I will be able to affect my health and the health of others.

This thinking will raise my vibrations.

Points to Ponder

There are only two ways to live your life. One is as though nothing is a miracle. The other is as though everything is a miracle.
—Albert Einstein

Life is either a daring adventure or nothing.
—Helen Keller

We die as we have lived. It is the fear of not having truly lived that makes us afraid to die.

Ignoring my passion is slow suicide.

I am not the object of experience but the silent observer within the experience itself.

We may sit in our library and yet be in all quarters of the earth.
—John Lubbock

When I judge another person, I do not define him or her. I merely define myself as someone who needs to judge.

A person does not need to be in the same room to be affecting me (mirror neurons).

> *Not all those who wander are lost.*
> —J. R. R. Tolkien

Do not become so busy collecting knowledge that there is not time to actually use it.

Nobody gives up anything deeply embedded in personality unless there is something of greater worth to take its place.

Clichés are just the truth that I am bored of, but they are still the truth.

> *The journey of a thousand miles starts with a single step.*
> —Lao Tse

Whatever I fight I strengthen. Whatever I resist will persist.

Life lived for tomorrow will always be a day away from being realized.

> *Believe those who are seeking truth. Doubt those who find it.*
> —Andre Gide

> *Men are most apt to believe what they least understand.*
> —Pliny the Elder

Points to Ponder

Thought can only *point* to the truth, but it never is the truth.

Facts are rare—it is mostly an opinion.

> *It's much more interesting to live not knowing than to have answers which might be wrong.*
> —Richard Feynman

It is better to know nothing than to know something that is not so.

Do I question my own ideas and beliefs as much as I do other people's ideas and beliefs?

> *It is good to have an end to journey toward; but it is the journey that matters in the end.*
> —Ernest Hemingway

Each day is not a step on the way to a destination; it is the destination.

The path is the way.

> *She filed a flight plan when she decided to lie and ended up in a crash even if someone else was at the controls when it happened.*
> —Red Mist (Patricia Cornwell)

> *Astrid isn't totally broken yet. But if a window could throw a brick at itself to test itself, that's what she'll do, she'll break herself, Magnus thinks, then she'll test how sharp she is by using her own broken pieces on herself.*
> —The Accidental Tourist (Anne Tyler)

Always appear to be eating with grace.

Lost time can never be found.

Ignorance and arrogance often go together.

It is easy to take off my clothes and have sex. People do it all the time. But opening up your soul to someone, letting them into your spirit, thoughts, fears, future, hopes, dreams ... that is being naked.
—Bob Bell

Grandiosity is always a cover for despair.

Failures are fingerprints on the road to achievement.

The person who does not make mistakes is unlikely to make anything.

Forever is composed of nows.
—Emily Dickenson

Alice: "How long is forever?" White Rabbit: "Sometimes, just one second."
—*Alice in Wonderland* (Lewis Carroll)

Quality requires attention.

My integrity is my standard.

Wisdom is knowing what to do next. Virtue is doing it.

Points to Ponder

Unless a man has learned to take orders, he can never learn to give them.

Notes from Air Force Colonel Mike:

- I never have to think about my rank; they should never forget it.
- There must be quality, quantity, time, and cost. Set a time limit.
- There must be consequences.
- I must hold them responsible for the jobs I assign them.
- I must *not* go and do it over—make them go back and do it.
- I must clarify *exactly* how I want the jobs done.

Our generation is realistic, for we have come to know man as he really is. After all, man is the being who invented the gas chambers of Auschwitz; however, he is also the being who entered those gas chambers upright, with the Lord's Prayer or the Shema Yisrael on his lips.
—Viktor Frankl

Do I believe in God because my parents do so, or do I believe in God because my friends do not?

Are heaven and hell, purgatory, and reincarnation only for people who believe in them?

If the founders of our religions came back, would they recognize their work?

Imagine Jesus that came back. Would he be a Baptist, a Catholic, a Greek Orthodox …?

> *Of all the communities available, the society of the true seeker is the only one I want to devote myself to.*
> —Albert Einstein

Am I a seeker? Seekers long for a better comprehension. Do I question myself as much as I question others? Do I question religion as much as science?

> *Money is numbers, and numbers never end. If it takes money to you happy, your search for happiness never ends.*
> —Julian in Los Arcos

Success is not defined by things.

> *Givers need to set limits because takers rarely do.*
> —Rachel Wolchin

Some people aren't loyal to me; they are loyal to their need of me. Once their need changes, so does their loyalty.

Why I bother myself with what they are doing. It is their thing, not mine.

Travel broadens the mind.

> *The world is a book and those who do not travel read only a page.*
> —Saint Augustine

Points to Ponder

Travel is more than the seeing of sights; it is a change that goes on, deep and permanent, in the ideas of living.
—Miriam Beard

Travel is fatal to prejudice, bigotry, and narrow-mindedness.
—Mark Twain

Travel makes one modest. You see what a tiny place you occupy in the world.
—Flaubert

A good traveler has no fixed plans and is not intent on arriving.
—Lao Tse

"Come to the edge," he said.
"We can't. We're afraid," they responded.
"Come to the edge," he said.
"We can't. We will fall," they responded.
"Come to the edge," he said.
And so they came.
And he pushed them.
And they flew.
—Guillaume Apollinaire

Lighten Up

I love people who make me laugh. It cures a multitude of ills.
—Audrey Hepburn

S mile first thing in the morning and get it over with.

When all else fails, put on a silly costume and sing a silly song.

We were just trying to pass for normal,
but we didn't know what normal was.
—Unknown

A positive attitude may not solve all my problems, but it will annoy enough people to make it worth the effort.

Imagination is everything.
It is the preview of life's coming attractions.
—Albert Einstein

If you love two people at the same time, choose the second one. Because if you really loved the first one, you wouldn't have fallen for the second.
—Johnny Depp

A toast: For all those who have me, the losers who lost me, and the lucky ones who will meet me.

I want an animal with the heart of a gentleman.

Mutation is utterly random, but selection is extremely choosy.
—Ursula Goodenough

Life is hard; it's even harder when you are stupid.
—John Wayne

When arguing with an idiot, a passer-by cannot tell the difference.
—Jan Rembowski

Artificial intelligence is no match for natural stupidity.

To argue with a person who has renounced the use of reason is like administering medicine to the dead.
—Thomas Paine

Stupidity is harmless. Intelligent stupidity is dangerous.

We don't stop playing because we grow old; we grow old because we stop playing.
—George Bernard Shaw

In living with a miserable person, how does a dog remain sane and joyous?

I'm sorry, dear, but in order for you to insult me, I must first value your opinion. Nice try, though.

> *I want to live a long time; I just don't want to get old.*
> —Emily Perepelecta

> *Always be yourself, unless you can be a unicorn; then always be a unicorn.*
> —Elle Lothlorien

Printed in the United States
By Bookmasters